How many times have you misspelled, mispronounced, or simply misused a word—and cringed in embarrassment over your error? It can be dauntingly difficult to remember the rules of grammar and usage, but this practical and witty guide makes it easier—and a lot more fun.

Keep *Miss Nomer's Guide to Painfully Incorrect English* within easy reach—and you'll not only sound smarter than ever before; you'll actually *be* smarter than ever before. It's the perfect guide for imperfect people who want to make fewer (not less!) mistakes.

Miss Nomer's Guide to Painfully Inc̶o̶r̶r̶e̶c̶t̶ English

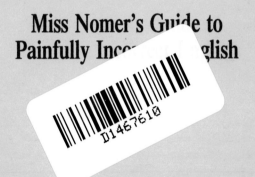

Miss Nomer's Guide to Painfully Incorrect English

*Because it's about time
you stopped sounding
like an imbecile.*

Alan Axelrod, Ph.D.

BERKLEY BOOKS, NEW YORK

For Anita and Ian.

MISS NOMER'S GUIDE TO PAINFULLY INCORRECT ENGLISH

A Berkley Book / published by arrangement with
the author

PRINTING HISTORY
Berkley edition / August 1998

The Penguin Putnam Inc. World Wide Web site address is
http://www.penguinputnam.com

ISBN: 0-425-16422-5

BERKLEY®
Berkley Books are published by The Berkley Publishing Group,
a member of Penguin Putnam Inc.,
200 Madison Avenue, New York, New York 10016.
BERKLEY and the "B" design
are trademarks belonging to Berkley Publishing Corporation.

PRINTED IN THE UNITED STATES OF AMERICA

10 9 8 7 6 5 4 3 2 1

Be Afraid. Be Very Afraid.

Most grammar, word, and style guides begin by telling you that they're all about more effective communication. Who can argue with that? Certainly not Miss Nomer. Read this book, and you may become a more effective communicator.

But there has never been a shortage of authors who promise to improve your English and build your vocabulary. Achieving the goal of speaking and writing more impressively is a commendable ambition that springs from healthy desires. It's like wanting to be neat, clean, well groomed, and freshly flossed.

Who can argue with that?

Yet consider the multibillion-dollar roll-on deodorant industry. It could never have been built on such a set of healthy desires. Roll-on deodorant is marketed not to people who want to smell good but to people who are afraid of smelling bad. Roll-on deodorant is sold as a cure for B.O., which men and women of a certain socioeconomic class (i.e., most of us) regard as a social *disease*. Miss Nomer has written this little book not to achieve a lofty but vague goal

of self-improvement but, more practically, as a cure for another social disease. She calls it V.O.: Verbal Odor.

The success of the roll-on deodorant industry proves that
we are all afraid we may stink. Aren't we also afraid that we
may sound stupid?

Most of us don't always want to go to the trouble of finding
the most elegant word, the most expressive word, or even
the *right* word, but we all want to avoid using the *wrong*
word—the word that brands us as ill-bred, poorly educated,
pitiful, and loathsome.

Is this an extreme position? Answer for yourself. Think
about the last time you heard someone say something like
this: "Irregardless, between you and I, I resent the inference." Then think about the last time you rode in an elevator
with a man or woman, sharply dressed and elegantly coiffed,
who just plain stank.

Miss Nomer's Guide to Painfully Incorrect English is a
high-spirited, frankly intolerant, and exuberantly prescrip-
tive index of the myriad malapropisms, usage errors,
grammatical blunders, mangled pronunciations, misspellings, and homonym snafus that most commonly torpedo discourse and make the speaker or writer look like a bloody
damn fool. *Miss Nomer's Guide to Painfully Incorrect English* rejects, utterly and without conscience, the politically
correct principle that has eviscerated every standard contemporary dictionary since *Webster's Third:* the perversely
holier-than-thou refusal to pass definitive judgment on
correct versus incorrect usage. "We live in a free and plu-
ralistic democracy," say the new grammarians and lexicog-
raphers, "in which it is our constitutional and moral right to
stink and sound stupid." If you agree with such linguistic
democracy, this book will only annoy you. Put it back on

the shelf. Miss Nomer sincerely hopes that you've saved your receipt.

But if you want to free yourself of verbal odor, if you want to ensure that you communicate not only effectively and intelligently but always *non-stupidly*, read on.

Unlike other grammar and usage books, which tell you that this or that is right, wrong, standard, nonstandard, awkward, and ugly, *Miss Nomer's Guide to Painfully Incorrect English* includes a painstakingly formulated VOQ (Verbal Odor Quotient) scale that rates the magnitude of each act of oral and written idiocy. The scale is expressed in negative numbers. Please commit it to memory:

- −1 This error will certainly raise an eyebrow.

- −2 This error will certainly raise the other eyebrow, too.

- −3 This error will certainly raise the hackles.

- −4 This error will certainly bring a judgment of utter imbecility.

- −5 This error will certainly ruin your life and destroy all that you have worked for.

Now, before you forge ahead with what promises to be a life-transforming reading experience, a word about Miss Nomer.

Who is she?

She is the one authority you can always trust. Her judgment is flawless. She is never wrong. She never lies. Beyond these facts, what more do you need to know?

Well, perhaps, you should know that "Miss Nomer" is

a fiction, a mouthpiece for Alan Axelrod, Ph.D., who has taught English composition and English and American literature at the University of Iowa, Mundelein College, Lake Forest College, and Furman University, and who is the author of more than twenty books on subjects ranging from American history to effective business and personal communication.

A

Most of us find this easy most of the time. The article *a* is used before words beginning with consonants and consonant sounds, and the article *an* is used before words beginning with vowels or vowel sounds, with one exception. *U* is certainly a vowel, but *u*—and all words beginning with a *yew* sound (for example *European*)—are preceded by *a* instead of *an*. *Y*, by the way, which sometimes masquerades as a vowel, always takes *a* as well: "It was *a* year to remember."

Sometimes things get a bit more complicated. Words beginning with *h*—certainly a consonant—seem to invite *an* instead of *a*: "The professor wrote *an* history of the Revolution." Nevertheless, the proper thing to do is to refuse the invitation. Use *a*: "Yes, he did write *a* history." Words such as *hour*, where the *h* is silent, should be treated as if they begin with the vowel, and *an* should be used. This leaves one other mystery: what to do when the article precedes certain abbreviations. For example: "Reginald studied hard and received *an* M.B.A." Or did he receive "*a* M.B.A."? Let your ear guide you here. *M* is pronounced *em* and, therefore, calls for *an* rather than *a*. In cases where the abbreviation is typically expanded when it is read, use the article appropriate to the way the word is actually read. "He was *a* N.J. state representative" would probably be read as "He was *a* New Jersey state representative," so anticipate this by using *a* rather than *an*.

abhor / deplore -3 VOQ

Often—and incorrectly—used interchangeably, these words actually have nothing in common, except that they are both used in unpleasant circumstances and may trace their origin to a Latin lineage. *Abhor* is rooted in the Latin verb form *abhorrere*, meaning "to shrink from," and that comes pretty close to summing up its modern meaning: to shun, to reject vehemently, to regard with loathing and horror (the latter word being derived from the second part of the Latin root: *horrere*, to shudder). *Deplore* is likewise ultimately derived from Latin, the word *deplorare*, to wail. The modern English word means to express strong disapproval of something or to condemn it. While one may *deplore* what one *abhors* and *abhor* what one *deplores*, it is also possible to *abhor* without deploring or to deplore without abhorring.

ability / capacity -2 VOQ

Often used interchangeably by careless folk, these words are not synonyms. *Ability* is the stronger, the more positive of the two words; for while a person can be born with either an *ability* or a *capacity* for something, only *ability* can be actively acquired. Moreover, *ability* suggests greater facility than mere *capacity*.

abjure / adjure -3.5 VOQ

These words belong to a select group of elegant terms that require intelligence to use and understand. If you're smart enough to use *abjure* and *adjure*, you should be smart enough to know the difference between them. Here it is: *Abjure* means to repudiate or renounce; the Latin *ab* prefix signifies "away" or "away from." *Adjure* means to entreat, to command, to direct earnestly; the Latin *ad* prefix means "to" or "toward."

able -4 VOQ

Able must not be used in passive constructions, like this: "He was *able* to be elected." Instead, write what you really mean: "He was *qualified for* election." Or "He *could be* elected." Or "He had a chance to win."

above / below -3 VOQ

Traditionally, *above* and *below* have been used to direct readers to cross-references and related material in books: "See Section 3, *above*." "Consult 'Important Exceptions,' *below*." Or "As mentioned *above* . . ." While some authorities accept *above* and *below* when the reference is precise, as in the first two examples cited, most object to the use illustrated in the third example. The safest course is simple: avoid *above* and *below* entirely. Alternatives include "cited later in the chapter," "as just discussed," "See Section 3 later in the chapter," "See 'Cautions' on page 65," and so on.

abridgement / abridgment -1 VOQ

U.S. spelling eliminates the *e* after the *g*.

absinth / absinthe -1.5 VOQ

Although you may encounter both spellings, you'll do well to adhere to the French original by including the final *e*.

absolutely -2 VOQ

This adverb means definitely, completely, without question, as in "I agree *absolutely*." It should not—*absolutely*, it should not—be used as a vague intensive, as in "This is an *absolutely* beautiful day."

a capella / a cappella -1.5 VOQ

The preferred spelling uses two *p*'s.

accept / except -4 VOQ

To *accept* is to receive, whereas to *except* is to exclude. *Accept* is always a verb, whereas *except* can be a verb, preposition, or conjunction: "I would talk to you, *except* that I don't like you." Or "I like everyone *except* you." To confuse *accept* and *except* is careless and just plain wrong. Don't do it.

acceptance / acceptation -4 VOQ

Acceptance—receiving something favorably or without protest—is rarely misused, but it is sometimes confused with *acceptation*, a word unusual enough to lead some to think it a coinage or non-word. But, odd sounding though it is, *acceptation* is a legitimate word. It means the way a word or phrase is commonly understood: "The *acceptation* of 'acquiese' is to comply with."

accompanied by / accompanied with -3 VOQ

Human beings are *accompanied by* other human beings, but things are *accompanied with* other things: "Gail was *accom-*

panied by Fred, who wore a dark suit *accompanied with* a vivid red shirt and tie.''

accouterment / accoutrement   -2 VOQ

Both spellings appear regularly, but some authorities consider *accoutrement* incorrect. Avoid it.

accrue   -1.5 VOQ

This is a fine financial and legal term: ''The interest continues to *accrue* on that loan, Mr. Hawkins.'' It should not be used as a synonym for *grow*: ''George just assumed his popularity would continue to *accrue*.''

acknowledgement / acknowledgment   -2 VOQ

The British spell this word with an *e* after the *g*. American editors find this especially annoying. Drop the *e*.

actionable   -3 VOQ

The word *actionable* has a very narrow meaning, denoting something that gives cause for legal proceedings: ''Calling me an embezzler is an *actionable* statement!'' Recent years have witnessed an epidemic of its use to denote anything capable of being acted upon or implemented—for example, ''Your ideas are feasible and therefore *actionable*.'' If you are using the word this way, stop it at once.

A.D. and B.C.   -2 VOQ

A.D., the abbreviation of the Latin *Anno Domini* (in the year of our Lord), is properly used before the year in question

and without a preposition: "Caligula was born A.D. 12."
(Not "*in* A.D. 12.") This is in contrast to B.C. (before Christ),
which should come after the year and does take the preposition *in*: "Julius Caesar was assassinated in 44 B.C."

While it is correct to use B.C. when speaking of one of the
centuries before the birth of Christ—"That ruler was active
in the third century B.C."—it is inappropriate to use A.D. in
this way, because it makes no sense to say "in the fifth
century in the year of our Lord." Make yourself clear by
always using B.C. to describe centuries before Christ, but simply give the century for those that came after Christ. Your
readers will understand that the "fifth century" is the fifth
century *after* Christ.

It should be noted that many scientists and social scientists, including some historians, reject the designations B.C.
and A.D. as anachronistic as well as chauvinistic or ethno-
centric. They suggest the somewhat more neutral B.C.E.—
before the Christian era—and C.E., which some (with sound
logic) insist stands for "Christian era" and others (with political correctness) claim stands for "common era." In either
case, these abbreviations correspond to B.C. and A.D.

adage / old adage   -3 VOQ

And now from the Department of Redundancy Department,
the expression *old adage*—"As the *old adage* says . . ." An
adage is an old saying, a bit of time-honored proverbial wisdom; the prefatory *old* is therefore superfluous.

adapter / adaptor   -2 VOQ

Quasi-technical words like this seem to invite the *-or* instead
of the *-er* ending, which seems somehow too commonplace

for the high-tech realm. Nevertheless, *-er* is the preferred ending here.

adduce / deduce / induce

See *deduce*.

adopt / assume   -2 VOQ

There is one case in which these words are almost—but, importantly, not quite—synonyms: in the sense of to take upon oneself. Consider: "Sarah *adopted* an attitude of indifference" versus "Sarah *assumed* an attitude of indifference." In the first sentence, it is likely that Sarah voluntarily chose the attitude of indifference, while, in the second sentence, one imagines that she is only pretending indifference. *Assume* implies pretense, while *adopt* implies choice.

adopted / adoptive   -2.5 VOQ

"Little Billy is an *adopted* child. Those are his *adoptive* parents." Use *adopted* to describe the child, *adoptive* to describe the parents who *adopted* him.

adverse / averse   -3.5 VOQ

These are two different adjectives. They are never interchangeable. *Adverse* is applied to unfavorable effects or events: "*Adverse* weather defeated Napoleon in Russia." To put it simply, *adverse* is synonymous with bad or unfavorable. *Averse* describes a person's opposition to something or a disinclination to do something: "I am *averse* to taking your mother to see *Cats*." For the phrase "I am *averse* to," you could readily substitute "I don't want to."

advertise / advertize   -2 VOQ

The *z* spelling is British and is to be shunned by loyal Americans.

advice / advise   -4 VOQ

Advice is a noun. *Advise* is a verb. Therein lies the critical difference between these two words. To *advise* is to give *advice*.

adviser / advisor   -2.5 VOQ

This is very frequently spelled with the *-or* ending, which somehow seems more official than the generic-seeming *-er*. But *-er* is preferred. Use it.

advocate / avocation   -3 VOQ

Careless pronunciation is probably responsible for the confusion between these totally unrelated terms. As a verb, *advocate* (the third syllable is pronounced "Kate") means to espouse, plead, or argue in favor of a cause or position. As a noun (the third syllable pronounced "kit"), the word denotes someone, such as an attorney, who advocates. An *avocation* is a hobby, a pursuit taken up in addition to one's vocation, or regular work.

aegis   -3.5 VOQ

The word is Latin for *shield* and implies protection: "Acting under the *aegis* of a court order, Acme Corporation persuaded its competitor to stop selling imitations of Acme products." *Aegis* is frequently manhandled, mauled, and generally abused as a synonym for *jurisdiction*: "That crime falls under the *aegis* of the State Supreme Court." (Well, some *do* complain that the courts exist to *protect* crime and criminals.)

aesthetic / esthetic -2 VOQ

The British tend to favor *esthetic*, but the standard U.S. spelling is *aesthetic*.

affect / effect -4 VOQ

Few commonly used words cause more confusion than these. In everyday usage, *affect* is a verb that means to influence or change—"The weather doesn't *affect* me at all"— whereas *effect* is usually a noun: "The weather has no *effect* on me at all." Less commonly, *effect* can be used as a verb meaning to cause or bring about—"We cannot *effect* a change in the weather"—and *affect* may mean to simulate or pretend: "I will try to *affect* pleasure." Less commonly still, *affect* is used as a noun that is synonymous with emotion or feeling. In this case, the *a* is pronounced as in "cat," the first syllable is strongly accented, and the word is used chiefly by psychologists. Indeed, it should be avoided in everyday speech.

afficionado / aficionado -2 VOQ

Officially, these are both acceptable variants, but some crusty old birds see the version with two *f*'s as a misspelling. Better avoid it.

affinity for   **-3 VOQ**

Affinity means kinship, sympathy, attraction, or fellow feeling; therefore, do not use the preposition *for* with it. *Affinity*
takes *between* or *with*. In some cases, *to* is also appropriate.

after the conclusion of   **-4 VOQ**

If you don't haul out the garbage regularly, everything starts
to stink. All you need to say or write is *after*: "*After* the
war . . ." rather than "*After the conclusion of* the war . . ."

afterward / afterwards   **-2.5 VOQ**

The British usually spell this with an *s* on the end. Americans
should not. Also see *toward / towards*.

aggravate / irritate   **-3 VOQ**

It is possible to live your entire life believing that these two
words are synonymous and therefore interchangeable. They
are not. To *aggravate* is to worsen an already bad or troublesome situation. To *irritate* is to annoy or to drive someone
to anger. "To *irritate* Miss Nomer by telling her that her
critical tone *aggravates* you will *aggravate* her already over-
bearing, overly demanding, and thoroughly sour disposition."

ago since   **-4 VOQ**

"It was ten years *ago since* we last saw one another" is a
dreadful little sentence. Use one or the other of these words,
but not both. If you choose *ago*, make certain the verb is in
the past tense: "It *was* ten years *ago* that we last saw one

another." If *since* is your choice, a present-tense verb is called for: "It *is* ten years *since* we last saw one another."

alibi

This is a splendid Latin word that (in Latin) means simply *elsewhere*. In English, it is properly used to mean a claim, plea, or fact of having been elsewhere when an offense was committed: "I couldn't have done it, Your Honor. I was with my mother-in-law at a performance of *Cats*." Too many speakers commit the misdemeanor of using *alibi* to denote an excuse or defense of any kind: "You always have an *alibi*." Another perfectly good word squandered!

all are / all is

It's hard to go wrong with *all*, which is an indefinite pronoun that may also function as a collective noun. In other words, it can take either a plural or a singular verb. Here is a familiar example of *all* as a collective noun: "*All is* lost!" If *all* is used to refer to individual things or people, it should be treated as a plural: "*All* (of us) *are* here."

alleged / accused / suspected

These words present a logical conundrum. When you read in the newspaper of an *alleged* murderer, an *accused* embezzler, or a *suspected* arsonist, you are reading of persons who do not exist. Under our system of law, a person is presumed innocent until found guilty through due process of law; therefore, news media must take care to hedge statements to avoid suit for libel or defamation. But, considered from the point of view of correct English usage, an *accused* embezzler *is*, in fact, an embezzler who has been *accused*, and a *suspected* arsonist is in fact an arsonist who is *suspected*. The case of *alleged* is somewhat different, since one cannot properly *allege* a person. What is *alleged* is a crime or a condition; thus a suspicious death may be classed as an *alleged* murder, but there is no such thing as an *alleged* murderer. It is also proper to express the quality of "allegedness" this way: "Smith was *alleged* to have murdered Johnson." Or "The prosecutor *alleged* that Smith murdered Johnson." All of this said, it is likely that we must accept the use of *alleged* to modify persons (*alleged* murderer, *alleged* spy, and so on), because of legal necessity; however, it is best to eschew the misuse of *accused* and *suspected*.

allude / elude   -4 VOQ

Be careful how you pronounce these similar-sounding words. To *allude* is to make indirect reference to something. To *elude* is to escape from or evade a pursuer. While the meanings of this pair are unrelated, both words are based on the Latin word *ludere* (to play). The Latin *alludere* means to play with, as if to suggest that one is toying with a meaning rather than approaching it with direct gravity. The Latin *eludere* suggests to play away from. One *eludes* a pursuer by cleverly "playing away from" him. The broken-field runner who successfully *eludes* would-be tacklers has played cleverly indeed.

allusion / illusion   -3 VOQ

An *illusion* is a mistaken or erroneous perception or belief, while an *allusion* is an indirect reference: "He made an unpleasant *allusion* to my having been deceived by an *illusion* of instant wealth." Miss Nomer has heard people speak of a "false illusion"; this is redundant—and very silly.

alongside of -2.5 VOQ

The addition of *of* makes for a highly annoying redundancy.
Delete it. Also note that *alongside* should be used only when
the dimension of length is involved: "The lumber lay *along-side* the garage wall." In all other cases, *beside* is called for:
"The cat lay *beside* the dog." But consider this: "The cat
was stretched out *alongside* the dog." In this case, the dimension of length is emphasized by "stretched out"; *alongside* is therefore appropriate. (But *beside* would also be
correct.) Also see *beside / besides.*

already / all ready -4 VOQ

Already deals with time. It means by this time or by a specified time: "They were *already* there when we arrived." Or
already may be synonymous with the phrase "so soon":
"Oh! You're here *already*!" *All ready* deals with preparedness. The word *all* merely intensifies the *ready*: "We are
all ready for you," which could just as easily be said, "We
are *ready* for you."

alright -3.5 VOQ

Among company that accepts *nite* for night and *lite* for light,
it may be all right to substitute *alright* for all right. Of course,
it's stupid and wrong to do so. But why let that bother you?

altar / alter -4 VOQ

Except among the pious, the word *altar* is not used every
day. Little wonder, then, that this focal point of religious
ceremony is often misspelled *alter*. Spelled that way, of
course, the word means to change or make different, to tailor

a garment to fit the wearer, or to spay a cat, dog, or other animal. Using *alter* when you mean *altar* is not a sin, but it is a spelling error only one degree removed from a catastrophe that will ruin your life.

alternately / alternatively   -2 VOQ

Alternately means one after the other. *Alternatively* means one or the other. "I could serve *alternately* as chairman and secretary; *alternatively,* we could elect a separate secretary."

altogether / all together   -3 VOQ

Altogether may mean entirely or completely: "I'm *altogether* pleased by your slavish devotion to the wisdom of Miss Nomer." The word may also mean with all included or counting: "*Altogether* a thousand fortunate people won." Finally, *altogether* may be used as synonym for on the whole or everything considered: "*Altogether*, you are lucky to be alive." Note that, when used to mean with all included, no comma separates the word from the number; however, a comma is required when the word is intended to mean on the whole.

    All together is about unity and unanimity: "*All together—* pull!" Or: "We did this work *all together*."

alumnus   -3 VOQ

Except in the case of some Ivy League holdouts, the marvelously indecipherable Latin has been replaced by stiffly starched English as diploma language; however, such terms as *alma mater* and *curriculum vitae* still survive, as does *alumnus*. The trouble is that gender is more important in Latin than it is in English. While most speakers thoughtlessly treat *alumnus* as a unisex word, it is proper to apply it only to a man. A female graduate is an *alumna*. The plural form *alumni* (the *i* is pronounced "eye") is likewise masculine; however, if you are referring to a mixed group of male and female graduates, this plural is acceptable. If your target consists exclusively of women, call them *alumnae* (the *ae* is pronounced "ee"). If you desperately fear being accused of sexism, use *both* plurals, "*alumni* and *alumnae*." While you won't be branded as sexist, you may be scorned as pedantic.

ambiguous / ambivalent   -3.5 VOQ

Fuzzy talkers use these interchangeably, even though they are by no means synonyms. *Ambivalent* is an adjective that describes conflicting feelings about or attitudes toward a goal, an idea, an object, or a person. "I am certainly not *ambivalent* about Miss Nomer's opinionated approach to the English language." *Ambiguous* is also an adjective, but that's where the similarity stops. Some authorities insist that the word may be applied only to written or spoken statements that have two or more possible meanings: "Miss Nomer is not unattractive." (Does this mean she's pretty or just not as ugly as some people have said of her? Is this a halfhearted compliment or an outright dig?) Others allow *ambiguous* to be applied to murky situations and confusing outcomes: "The poll results are *ambiguous*. Although 100 percent of those polled said that they obey Miss Nomer without question and are intensely grateful for her advice, the respondents were unanimous that they would never invite her to a cocktail party."

amend / emend   -3 VOQ

To *amend* is to improve or correct a statement, document, rule, law, or policy in a general or broad sense. To *emend* is

to edit, critically and specifically, a written text. When the
framers of the Constitution decided to *amend* the document
by the addition of the Bill of Rights, they greatly improved
it. (Presumably, some poorly paid but duly patriotic editor
had been hired earlier to *emend* the work by correcting Thomas Jefferson's careless spelling.)

amiable / amicable   -2.5 VOQ

Two adjectives here. *Amiable* describes a friendly, pleasant,
and congenial person, whereas *amicable* describes a relationship that is characterized by the absence of strife, enmity,
and hard feelings and by the presence of general peacefulness
and goodwill.

among / between

See *between / among*.

among other things   -2 VOQ

This tired phrase all too often rolls into speech both spoken
and written. At the very least, it is meaninglessly vague: "I
object to your being tardy, *among other things*." At worst,
it is just plain nonsense: "He was a Supreme Court justice,
among other things." This distinguished jurist was a *thing*?
The single most effective way to sharpen speech and writing
is to make it precise, full of action, events, facts, and obser-
vations—not vague and empty verbiage.

amongst   -3 VOQ

To American ears this Briticism sounds objectionably archaic
and quaint. Expunge it from your vocabulary, and use *among*
instead.

amoral / immoral

See *immoral / amoral.*

amount / number -4 VOQ

Like many other common words, *amount* has multiple meanings. Among these is a sense synonymous with *quantity*:
"She has a large *amount* of brains or wit or courage or arrogance or salt or pepper or chicken fat." Note that these are
all aggregate, bulk substances or abstract qualities. The word
amount goes with these. Obviously, the word *number* cannot
be used here—"She has a large number of brains or wit or
courage or arrogance or salt or pepper or chicken fat"—and
no speaker of idiomatic English would make such a mistake.
However, many people use *amount* when *number* is called
for: "There were a large *amount* of people there." As *number* cannot be applied to bulk or abstract quantities, so
amount cannot be used to enumerate individuals. Here *number* is appropriate: "She has a large *number* of friends or
enemies or paper dolls or saltshakers or pepper mills or bot-
tles of chicken fat."

amuck / amok -1.5 VOQ

Some dictionaries give *amuck* as an alternate spelling of
amok, while a few authorities actually favor *amuck* as the
preferred spelling. They are in the minority, however. Use
amok.

anaesthesia / anesthesia -2 VOQ

The *ae* in the first spelling was once a ligature: the two letters
were joined, like this—æ. But no more. The *ae* spelling is

favored in Britain, but seems affected or old-fashioned on the U.S. side of the ocean. Spell this word *anesthesia*.

analog / analogue   -3 VOQ

Analog hasn't been spelled with the *-ue* tacked onto the end for a very long time. In this computer-driven age, the older spelling is unacceptable. Write *analog*.

antiseptic / sterile

See *sterile / antiseptic*.

anxious / eager   -2 VOQ

Even otherwise decently turned-out and well-scrubbed people use these interchangeably, and our language suffers. *Anxious* is an unhappy word, the adjectival counterpart of *anxiety*. Use the word in the sense of worry, apprehension, foreboding, uneasiness, and fear. Use *eager* to convey enthusiastic impatience, keen desire, ardent feeling, a sense of looking forward to something or some event with pleasure. "I am *anxious* about the results of my grammar test" is perfectly legitimate. "I am *anxious* to get the results of my English usage exam" means that you dread the likely results, but "I am *eager* to get the results of my English usage exam" proclaims to the world your confidence in the anticipated outcome. Miss Nomer strongly recommends that the next time your significant other confides sweetly that he or she is *anxious* to see you, demand the right to administer an English usage exam.

any and all -4 VOQ

Be not prodigal with thy words. Use *any* or *all,* but not *any and all.* "We will take *any and all* suggestions" is a wasteful sentence. Except in cases where clarity of meaning makes it necessary to include explicitly *any, some,* and *all,* exercise choice.

any are / any is -0 VOQ

This one's free. *Any* is an indefinite pronoun and functions as a collective noun. It can take either a plural or a singular verb: "*Any* help *is* appreciated, and *any* suggestions *are* welcome."

anyways -5 VOQ

This is a ghastly illiteracy that, uttered unintentionally, brands the user as a fugitive from television fare of the *Leave It to Beaver* vintage. Some people who know better employ the word on purpose, in order to sound cuddly cute. Miss Nomer has found that these people seldom advance along the path of their chosen career and eventually are forced to scrape by in a shabby hotel room, heating a can of condensed soup over a blue Sterno flame, neon sign flashing through the dust-coated window. Please: the right word is *anyway,* or use such phrases as *in any case* or *in any event*.

anywheres -5 VOQ

This, too, is illiterate. Drop the *s*.

aphrodisiac / aphrodisiacal -3 VOQ

We all know that *aphrodisiac* is a noun, but some doubters decline to believe that it can also serve as an adjective. It was most likely one of these people who invented *aphrodisiacal*. The word won't work. Discard it and use *aphrodisiac* as noun as well as adjective: "Oysters are supposed to have an *aphrodisiac* effect."

apogee / perigee -3 VOQ

These terms have been borrowed into general usage from astronomy, in which *apogee* is the farthest point from earth of the lunar orbit, and *perigee* is the closest point. Taking this sense a little beyond astronomy, those who launch rockets refer to the highest point of a suborbital missile's trajectory as its *apogee*. There is no corresponding *perigee*, since the lowest point a suborbital missile reaches is the earth. *Kaboom.* The two terms are also used figuratively: "Dr. Smithson reached the *apogee* of her career when she developed a cure for self-doubt. Her career's *perigee* came with the discovery that her medical degree had been obtained fraudulently."

apprehend / comprehend -2 VOQ

These terms are closely related. Both mean *understand*, but to *apprehend* is to reach an understanding largely through intuitive means, while to *comprehend* is to understand with a firm grasp and on a rational or intellectual level.

apprise / apprize / appraise -2.5 VOQ

To *apprise* is to give notice of: "Please *apprise* me of any change in your situation." To *apprize* is to value or appreciate: "I greatly *apprize* you as my friend." It is actually easy to avoid confusing *apprise* with *apprize* if you recognize the word *prize* within the second term. "I *prize* your friendship" is synonymous with "I apprize your friendship." Now that you've learned how to avoid this error, note that *apprize,* almost an archaism, is rarely used in any case. It is true, however, that *apprise* is frequently misspelled with a *z.* A greater danger is confusion between *apprise* and *appraise*, which means to evaluate, to judge the value of, to set a valuation or price: "The jeweler *appraised* the engagement ring you gave me at a big fifty bucks."

apt / liable / likely   -2 VOQ

Many otherwise prudent people are prodigal in their use of these three words, which they regard as synonyms: "I'm *apt* to see you there." "I'm *liable* to see you there." "I'm *likely* to see you there." It is true that all three describe states of likelihood, but beyond this general similarity, their specific meanings are quite distinct. *Apt* suggests that its subject has some natural tendency enhancing the probability of a certain outcome: "You have such musical genius that you are *apt* to become an accordion virtuoso." *Liable* strongly implies adversity. In fact, its proper and most effective use is governed by this rule: *Liable* is used when the subject will probably be affected adversely by the action described in the infinitive verb. An example will make this clear: "Fred, if you sit on it, that accordion is *liable* to break." Here *accordion* is the subject, and *to break* is the infinitive. Finally, the word *likely* is the most general of these terms and can be applied universally. However, don't pass up the opportunity to use the more vivid and specific *apt* and *liable* when these are truly called for. Also see *liable / libel*.

arbiter / arbitrator / mediator   -3.5 VOQ

Reckless individuals use these terms interchangeably. A mistake. An *arbiter* is one who may judge, ordain, or decree at will. An arbiter of fashion, for example, is not obliged to give reasons for his decisions. *Arbitrator* describes someone who functions very nearly as a judge; however, unlike a judge, the *arbitrator* is not installed in office by due process of law, but is usually chosen by the principal parties in a dispute. The *arbitrator* hears evidence from the disputants and makes a decision. In contrast, a *mediator* does not function as a judge at all, but hears out the disputants and attempts, through reason and persuasion, to bring them to agreement. *Arbitrate* is derived from a Latin root meaning to give judgment, whereas the Latin root of *mediate* means to be in the middle. Looking to these roots will help you use these words correctly.

archaeology / archeology   -2 VOQ

Most Americans prefer spelling the more streamlined version of a word—*encyclopedia* instead of *encyclopaedia*, for example. In the case of *archaeology*, however, the older, more complex spelling is preferred, even by Americans, perhaps because *archaeology* deals with old and complex things.

archetype / archetypal / archetypical   -3 VOQ

The most irritating abuse these words suffer is mispronunciation as ''arch-type'' and ''arch-typal.'' *Archetype* has three syllables, not two. The first syllable is pronounced ''ar,'' and the second ''ki,'' with a short *i* as in *kit*. The third is ''type,'' pronounced like *type*. As for the third word in this list, it is also a source of irritation, because it is not a word at all. Use *archetypal*, not *archetypical*.

Beyond these basic irritants, there is the excessively loose application of *archetype* and *archetypal* when words such as *typical* or *characteristic* would be far more appropriate. "Officer Krupke was the *archetypal* cop." Maybe. More probably, however, he was "a *typical* cop." Reserve *archetype* and *archetypal* to describe the original model or example after which subsequent things of the kind are patterned. These words may also be used to describe an ideal type or quintessence. In the psychology of Carl Gustav Jung (1875–1961), *archetype* has a special and widely accepted meaning as an instinctive pattern that has a universal character and that is expressed in behavior, words, and images. Please take a look at *prototype / archetype* as well.

Arctic / Antarctic   -4 VOQ

Inasmuch as these two vast land masses are at opposite ends of the earth, confusing one with the other may be a rather serious matter. The *Arctic* is a region of the Northern Hemisphere between the North Pole and the northern timberlines of North America and Eurasia. The *Antarctic* is a region of the Southern Hemisphere that may properly be called Antarctica, a continent lying mostly within the *Antarctic* Circle and irregularly centered on the South Pole. Note that *arctic*—with a lowercase *a*—may be used as a general adjective to describe extreme coldness: "The weather in Minneapolis is often *arctic*." Finally, be aware that a mush-mouthed pronunciation of *Arctic* often results in the misspelling *Artic* and that the same sloppiness may produce *Anartic*.

ardors   -3 VOQ

As the plural of *ardor*, *ardors* legitimately refers to passions; however, through a misperceived connection with *arduous* (meaning difficult, rigorous), the word is often misused as a synonym for rigors, difficulties, labors, or travails: "He rested from the *ardors* of his long travels." Wrong.

Argentinean   -1 VOQ

. . . but-5 VOQ if spoken to a citizen of Argentina. You'll find *Argentinean* in the dictionary, but people from Argentina far prefer to be called *Argentine* (the final syllable is pronounced to rhyme with "fine"). It is best to cultivate the habit.

artsy / arty   -3 VOQ

Many find both of these words objectionable—worthy of a Philistine, not a cultivated person. If you must use one of these, choose *arty*.

as   -1 VOQ

Like so many of the simplest words in English, *as* has several meanings. Kindly glance at the entry for *like / as,* which contains a discussion about when to use one or the other. Here let's look at a common application of *as*, which some people find objectionable: the use of the word as a synonym for *because* or *since*: "*As* I am president of the club, my word is law." Miss Nomer is at a loss to explain why this use of *as* raises the occasional eyebrow, but it does. Among strangers, you are advised to avoid it and to use *because* or *since* instead.

ascendant / ascendent   -1.5 VOQ

Either is acceptable, but *ascendant* edges out *ascendent* as
the slightly preferred spelling.

as per / per

See *per / as per*.

assassin, would-be   -4 VOQ

The phrase is a familiar one—*would-be assassin*—but frequency of use does not make it any more meaningful. An
assassin is a person who kills or attempts to kill through
treachery. Thus *would-be* is redundant. It is also nonsensical,
because the role of *assassin* is not a status to which anyone
would aspire.

assess / impose   -3 VOQ

The word means to evaluate or, applied to taxation or law,
it means to apportion or levy a tax or to impose a fine. Unfortunately, *assess* is frequently misused as a synonym for
imposed, without the qualification of a tax or fine. "The
judge *assessed* a fine" is correct, but "The judge *assessed*
a jail term" is wrong.

assume / presume   -2.5 VOQ

These words differ more in degree than in kind. To *assume*
is, essentially, to take for granted without evidence or without evaluating the evidence. To *presume* is somewhat less
arrogant. It expresses a belief that something is true, based
on prevailing circumstances, experience, or common sense.

"Let's *assume* the first phase of the project succeeds. I *presume* you will agree that we will need a fully developed follow-up plan."

assure / ensure / insure   -3 VOQ

Three variations on the root word *sure*: To *assure* is to make someone sure of something, as in "I *assure* you, the *Titanic* is a safe ship." To *ensure* is to make certain or make safe: "*Ensure* that you wear your life jacket." And to *insure* is to provide or obtain insurance to protect life or property or other assets financially: "*Insure* your life generously before you set sail."

astonish / surprise

See *surprise / astonish.*

astringent / strident / stringent

See *stringent / astringent / strident.*

astronomic / astronomical   -2 VOQ

Astronomical is preferred to *astronomic* in such figurative phrases as "*astronomical* expenses." In matters actually relating to astronomy, *astronomical* is not just preferred, it is required.

atheist / agnostic   -4 VOQ

No, *agnostic* is not a fancy word for *atheist.* The two terms denote different degrees of belief—or nonbelief—in a deity. *Agnostic* is based in the Greek word for knowledge. Put the *a* prefix in front of it, and you signify an absence of knowledge. *Agnostic* literally means without knowledge or does not know, and it describes a person who does not know whether God exists. Put the same prefix in front of *theist*—which is derived from *theos*, the Greek word for god—and you have a person without a God. *Agnostics* do not know whether God exists, whereas *atheists* believe God does not exist.

attenuate   -5 VOQ

It is a sad truth that the social sciences, particularly psychology, have long been marred by the use of bland and turgid language. In the worst instances, perfectly good English words are also tortured into new and utterly unfounded meanings. *Attenuate* means to make slender or small, to reduce or weaken, or to reduce the density of. In the field of immunology, *attenuate* means to make a strain of virus or bacteria less virulent—so that it can be used as a vaccine, for example. In electronics, to *attenuate* a signal is to reduce its amplitude without creating distortion. These two specialized meanings are both clearly related to the general-use meanings of the word. However, some psychologists use *attenuate* as a synonym for "to pay attention" or "to direct attention toward." Even in a civilization where some suffering souls fork over $250 an hour for the privilege of lying on a couch in an analyst's office, such blatant theft of meaning is unacceptable.

at this time   -1.5 VOQ

Reduce this to a single word, *now*. Your readers and listeners will receive it as a blessing. Also see *present time, at the.*

attorney / lawyer / counsel / counselor   -1.5 VOQ

Lawyer is the most general term for one fully qualified to practice law. *Attorney* actually denotes a person who is designated by another to transact certain business on his behalf—hence the phrase *power of attorney* for a legal document designating such a proxy. An *attorney* may or may not be a *lawyer* (although in the United States he or she almost always is). *Counsel* is a legalistic term for *lawyer* and is usually reserved for official communications in court or in correspondence that bears legal weight. *Counsel* is often used in official job titles: Rhonda Blank, corporate *counsel*. *Counselor* is typically used in court and between one *lawyer* and another.

auger / augur   -3 VOQ

Why these words should be so similar is beyond even Miss Nomer. As a noun, *auger* is the name of a tool used to bore into wood or into the earth. It is generally much larger than a drill. The word may also be used as a verb to describe the act of using an auger. Pilots, in their colorful way, speak of *augering in* to describe an earth-piercing crash. Spelled with a second *u* in place of the *e*, the word means to foretell the future or to use various signs and omens in an effort to foretell the future. Most commonly, *augur* is used as a transitive verb meaning to serve as an omen or to betoken some outcome—for example, ''Generally rising rents *augur* the gentrification of the neighborhood.'' Frequently, the word is used in combination with *well*: ''That the theater was occupied by only three people, including the playwright and his family, does not *augur well* for a profitable run.'' Far less commonly, *augur* is used as a noun synonymous with *prophet* or *soothsayer* and may also be applied to the original ancient Roman religious officials whose job it was to predict the future on the basis of omens.

aural / oral   -4 VOQ

These words are pronounced identically, but they have different meanings. *Aural* refers to the sense of hearing. *Oral* refers to the mouth or spoken speech. Take a look at *oral / verbal*.

auspicious / propitious / propitiate   -2 VOQ

That two of these rather succulent words rhyme does not make any of them synonyms. *Auspicious* means favorable or promising, and it is usually applied to some momentous undertaking, such as the commencement of a major project or enterprise: "The presence of so many rock stars at the grand opening was *auspicious*." *Propitious* is similar, also suggesting favorable disposition, but it is usually applied to less momentous events. *Auspicious* suggests the more or less mystical presence of good omens, whereas *propitious* is more practical: "The presence of so many rock stars at the grand opening was *propitious*. Otherwise, the event would have been stuffy and boring."

While *auspicious* and *propitious* differ significantly in connotation, *propitiate* is an entirely different word from either of these. Indeed, whereas *auspicious* and *propitious* are adjectives, *propitiate* is a verb. It means to conciliate or to appease some great power, usually a deity: "The ancients offered human sacrifices to *propitiate* the gods." And that was certainly neither an *auspicious* event nor a *propitious* circumstance for the person lying on the altar.

avenge / revenge   -1 VOQ

Both of these words may be used as verbs meaning to inflict punishment or penalty in response to some wrong or injury suffered or to inflict such retribution on behalf of someone else. "Hamlet sought to *avenge* (or to *revenge*) the murder of his father." Or "Hamlet sought to *avenge* (or to *revenge*) his murdered father." Note, however, that *avenge* sounds more natural as a verb than does *revenge*, which strikes the ear as more appropriate when it is used as a noun to denote the act of vengeance: "Living well is the best *revenge*." Using *revenge* as verb, while correct, may induce a cocked eyebrow, which will distract a hearer or reader from your message. Give preference to *avenge* as a verb and to *revenge* as a noun. Do note that, unlike *revenge, avenge* is exclusively a verb.

average / mean / median   -4 VOQ

It's about time somebody stepped in to sort out these three *different* terms. The *average* is the sum of a series divided by the number of members in the series: "Three students scored 65, 75, and 90 on the exam. The average score was 77." (Actually, it was 76.66666666667, but Miss Nomer rounded it off.) The *mean* is the middle point. If the low score was 65 and the high 90, the mean score is 77.5, which is midway between these two numbers. A *mean* takes into account only the highest (greatest) and lowest (least). The *median* is the point in a series where half the members are on one side and half are on the other: The median of 65, 75, and 90 is 75. If you need proof that *average, mean*, and *median* denote different things, look at the results: 77, 77.5, and 75.

avert / avoid   -2.5 VOQ

This pair is dangerous because either word "sounds right" in most cases. Be aware, however, that to *avert* is to prevent or fend off, whereas to *avoid* is to eschew, shun, or otherwise turn away from. "The bridge had collapsed, but we *averted* disaster by *avoiding* Bridge Road that evening."

awestricken / awestruck   -3.5 VOQ

It is true that a past participle of *struck* is *stricken* and that *stricken* is also the adjectival form of *struck*; nevertheless, *awestruck* has no separate participle or adjectival form. Use *awestruck* for the past, past participle, and adjectival forms: "I had been *awestruck* (not *awestricken*) by his display of knowledge." Or "She was an *awestruck* (not *awestricken*) young woman."

axe / ax   -1 VOQ

Trying to decide which of these to use? Americans prefer to drop the *e*.

ay / aye   -2 VOQ

All in favor say . . . *aye*.

B

backward / backwards
-2 VOQ

In America we move *backward*, but in England they move *backwards*.

bad / badly
-4 VOQ for misusing *bad*
-2 VOQ for "feel badly"

Okay. Here it is: *bad* is an adjective, and *badly* is an adverb. This means that *bad* modifies nouns, while *badly* modifies verbs. "We need more money *bad*" is illiterate, because *need* is a verb. (The correct form: "We need more money *badly*.") Or this: "His head ached *bad*." *Ached* is a verb and therefore needs an adverb. (Like this: "His head ached *badly*.") But here's an interesting twist. How many times have you heard a self-consciously genteel (or simply pretentious) person say "I feel *badly* about that"? While some authorities find this acceptable, it will provoke objections. True enough, *feel* is a verb, and, in similar expressions, an adverb is perfectly acceptable: "I feel strongly about that." However, by tradition, "feel *badly*" implies a physical problem, as if the speaker has calluses on his fingers and, quite literally, feels *badly*. The universally accepted expression—when you intend "feel" to express an emotion—is "I feel *bad*."

barefoot / barefooted -2 VOQ

Do not go *barefooted* into that good night? Ridiculous! Do not go *barefoot*.

basilisk / odalisque -4 VOQ

A *basilisk* is a legendary dragon whose breath or merest glance can kill. The word has been borrowed to denote real animals, representatives of the genus *Basiliscus*, which includes lizards found in the tropical Americas. In jarring contrast, an *odalisque* is a concubine or female harem slave.

bastard / illegitimate child (daughter, son) / natural child (daughter, son) -4 VOQ (*bastard*),
-4 VOQ (*illegitimate*),
-0 VOQ (*natural*)

Some misguided curmudgeons condemn *natural child, natural daughter*, and *natural son* as euphemisms for *bastard* or *illegitimate child*; however, expressions using *natural* are preferable to *bastard* or expressions using *illegitimate*, which unfairly denigrate the offspring in a manner that mainstream society now finds unacceptable. Also see *love child*.

baud rate -3 VOQ

Those who are eager to demonstrate their computer literacy freely use the phrase *baud rate* to describe the speed at which a computer modem transmits data. Beware! Such a statement is computer *illiteracy*. In most cases, *bps (bits per second)* is the term you should use.

Baud, named in honor of the French electrical engineer

Jean Maurice Émile Baudot (1845–1903), is a measure of the rate at which electric signals are modulated (changed). For example, an ordinary telephone line can accommodate 2,400 signal changes per second and thus has a baud rate of 2,400. Today's high-speed modems encode more than a single data bit (a *bit* being the smallest unit of meaningful data, at least as far as a computer is concerned) in each signal change. A marginally respectable modem, for example, encodes 12 data bits in each signal change. Its baud rate is still 2,400 (that's all ordinary analog telephone lines can handle), but it transmits 28,800 bits per second (bps), or 12 data bits per signal change at a rate of 2,400 signal changes per second: $12 \times 2400 = 28,800$. Poseurs who wish to wrap themselves in an aura of fashionable techno-nerdiness unwittingly use *baud* and *bps* as synonyms. However, *bps* and *baud* are two different things. The *bps* rate is the number of data bits per signal multiplied by the *baud rate.* In the old days—say, circa 1985—few modems climbed above 2,400 *bps* and were content to transmit one data bit per signal change; therefore, the *baud rate* and *bps* rate were functionally the same. If you are still chugging along on a 1,200 or 2,400 bps modem, your computer-savvy friends probably shun you anyway, so it hardly matters if you confuse *baud rate* and *bps.* But if you own state-of-the-art hardware, you'd better learn to talk the talk and avoid those ugly behind-your-back expressions of contempt that are eroding your authority at the office and, sooner or later, will cause even your children and household pets to turn against you.

B.C. and A.D.

See *A.D. and B.C.*

beast / brute   -1 VOQ

A *beast* is any large four-footed animal. Secondarily, the word may denote a contemptible person who exhibits brutality and stupidity. In this second sense, the word comes close to *brute*; however, *brute* should not be applied to animals.

because / since   -2.5 VOQ

These words are used interchangeably far too often. Think of it this way: *because* means for the reason that, while *since* is the equivalent of inasmuch as. Use *because* when you want most directly to express cause and effect. Use *since* when the relationship is less direct. "I won't buy that purse for you *because* it is ugly." "*Since* you don't seem to like that purse very much, I won't buy it for you." Note that *since* is often put at the beginning of a sentence, as the first word of an introductory clause. In contrast, many stylists consider the use of *because* to introduce a sentence bad form.

behalf   -1 VOQ

In behalf of or *on behalf of*? That is the question. Few users care, but *in behalf of* should be used in the sense of "for the benefit of," while *on behalf of* means "as an agent of" or "in place of." "*On behalf of* the citizens of Wetville, the council members raised funds *in behalf of* the flood victims."

behaviors   -3 VOQ

Unless you make a living as a psychologist or educator, rendering *behavior* as a plural must grate on the nerves. *Behavior* is a collective noun and does not require a plural form:

"This kind of *behavior*—kicking, screaming, shouting—is not acceptable, even from a grammarian." Avoid "These *behaviors*—kicking, screaming, shouting—are not acceptable, even from a grammarian." If you must emphasize the sense of plurality, use the phrase "types of *behavior*."

bellboy   -5 VOQ

Bellboy is demeaning and must be avoided. Use *bellman* or, if appropriate, *bell captain*. The politically correct among us might insist on *bell person*, but, in her many travels, Miss Nomer has yet to meet a female member of the bell staff. Perhaps the safest course is the old standby *bellhop*.

below / above

See *above / below*.

beside / besides   -4 VOQ

Beside means next to, in comparison with ("This car seems like a good value *beside* the others in its price range") or on an equal footing with ("This car has earned a place *beside* others of its class for its reputation as a good value"). *Besides* means in addition to—"Many people *besides* Miss Nomer speak admirable English." *Besides* may also be used in three other senses from which *beside* is barred. *Besides* may mean furthermore or moreover: "*Besides*, Miss Nomer is hardly alone in her desire to raise the standards of English usage." The word may mean otherwise or else: "In addition to language pundit, Miss Nomer has been a sushi chef, but nothing else *besides*." Finally, *besides* may mean other than: "No one *besides* Miss Nomer knows the secret of the Phantom Grammarian." Also see *alongside of*.

bespoke / bespoken -3 VOQ

Both of these words are rare on the U.S. side of the Atlantic but common in England, where a *bespoke* suit is a custom-made suit, in contrast to one bought, ready-made, off the rack. The proper term for such a garment is *bespoke,* not *bespoken.*

be sure and -3 VOQ

For reasons that elude Miss Nomer, the word *and* is often made to substitute for *to* in this and similar utterances: "Be sure *and* see me before you leave." Why not use *to*, the right word? It's shorter!

betterment -2 VOQ

Carelessly used as a synonym for improvement, *betterment* actually has specifically social implications, as in the "*betterment* of slum conditions" or "Cesar Chávez worked for the *betterment* of life among migrant laborers." Avoid using the word in situations where *improvement* is called for: "The push-button telephone represents a *betterment* of the rotary dial telephone."

between / among -2.5 VOQ

"There is no trouble *between* you and me" is a fine sentence. "There is no trouble *between* the three of us" is not. *Between* is used in cases involving two objects. If more than two objects are involved, use *among*: "There is no trouble *among* the three of us." And, please, see the entry *I / me* for some straight talk about the objective case.

bi- / semi-   -4 VOQ

These prefixes cause a great deal of confusion. Force yourself
to remember that *bi-* means *two* and that *semi-* means *half*;
therefore, *biweekly* is every two weeks ("two-weekly," as it
were), and *semiweekly* is twice a week ("half weekly"). But
take a look at *biannual / biennial*, the next entry.

biannual / biennial   -2 VOQ

Biannual means twice a year, whereas *biennial* means every
two years. *Semiannual* is a synonym for *biannual*. End of
story.

bias   -3 VOQ

Bias cannot stand alone. It must carry a modifying phrase,
as in "President Kennedy had a *bias* against Fidel Castro."
Or "I hold a *bias* in favor of men with plenty of money."
"In the 1960s, a number of southern governors were guilty
of *bias*" contains more than a grain of truth, but it is grammatically incorrect. The governors were "guilty of *discrimination*," or they were "guilty of *bias* against
African-Americans in general and integration in particular."
And please take note that *bias* can be against or in favor of;
it is not, in itself, a negative term.

bisect / dissect   -3 VOQ

To *bisect* is to divide a thing into two parts, usually equal
parts. To *dissect* is to cut a thing into pieces with the object
of investigating its component parts. Most often this is applied to biological specimens that are carefully cut apart for
scientific or educational purposes.

bizarre / bazaar -3 VOQ

Given the similarity with which they are pronounced, there is nothing *bizarre* about the confusion between these two words. *Bizarre* means strange, unusual, weird, or freakish. A *bazaar* is a marketplace or a charity event at which contributed articles are sold in order to raise money. The word originally denoted street markets in the Middle East.

blatant / flagrant -2.5 VOQ

The adjective *blatant* means completely obvious, sometimes with the added connotation of offensiveness, vulgarity, obtrusiveness, or crassness. *Flagrant* always means obviously and conspicuously offensive. It is used to describe outrageous violations of commonly accepted standards of decent or moral or humane behavior.

blind -2 VOQ

Use this word as an adjective to describe a person with total vision loss only. For those whose vision loss is partial, use *visually impaired* or *visually challenged*.

boat / ship -3 VOQ

Don't tell the captain of an aircraft carrier that you like his *boat*. All large vessels are properly called *ships*, with the exception of submarines, which, no matter how large, are called *boats*. The only other naval vessels that may be called *boats* are PT *boats* and gun*boats*. Such craft as motor launches and life*boats* are also properly described as boats. Everything else is a *ship*.

born / borne   -4 VOQ

Be careful with these. *Born* is a verb meaning brought into
life by birth or simply brought into being—an idea, for example, may be *born*. The word can also be used to describe
someone who has a particular natural ability: "She is a *born*
singer." *Borne* is a past participle of the verb *bear,* which
means to carry or to endure: "He *bears* a heavy load" or
"He has *borne* a heavy load." "She *bears* great grief" or
"She has *borne* great grief." *Borne* is often applied as a
suffix to other words to mean transmitted by or transported
by: "Colds are transmitted by air*borne* viruses."

Brahma / Brahman / Brahmin   -1 VOQ

Brahma is the Hindu creator god, one of a triad also consisting of Shiva and Vishnu. The god's name may also be
spelled *Brahman*. *Brahma* or *Brahman* is also the word for
a prayer, for a source of sacred power, and for the absolute
being. Spelled *Brahmin*—and sometimes *Brahman*—the
word signifies the first of the four Hindu classes or castes; a
Brahmin is responsible for officiating at various religious cer-
emonies and for studying and teaching the Vedas, or Hindu
holy books. *Brahmin* is the preferred spelling for the figurative extension of this term, applied to a member of the
socially elite class of New Englanders descended from the
oldest of the region's families. Most often these people are
called *Boston Brahmins*. *Brahma* or *Brahmin* is the preferred
spelling for the breed of cattle developed in the American
Southwest from stock that originated in India: "a *Brahma*
(or *Brahmin*) bull."

breach / breech   -3 VOQ

Breach may be a noun or a verb. As a noun, it means an opening, tear, or rupture. By metaphorical extension, it may mean a violation (a rupture) of an agreement, trust, promise, or contract. As a verb, to *breach* is to tear, rupture, or force an opening in something: "The army laid siege to the castle, planning to *breach* the wall." It may also be used in the figurative sense: "I don't want to *breach* our agreement." A special meaning of the verb *breach* familiar to readers of Herman Melville's *Moby-Dick* is the leap of a whale out of the water. It is also proper—and colorful—to speak of waves *breaching* (*breaking*) on the shore.

While *breach* is derived from Old and Middle English words for *break, breech* is rooted in *brec*, the Old English plural of *broc*, which signifies a leg covering such as hose or trousers. In modern English, the word *breeches* (usually pronounced and often spelled "britches") is testament to the root. *Breech,* however, refers part of what *breeches* cover: the lower rear portion of the trunk, the buttocks. (In a *breech* birth, the baby's feet and buttocks emerge before the head.) By figurative extension, *breech* also refers to the part of a firearm behind the barrel: the weapon's rear end.

bring to a head   -1.5 VOQ

It is a source of wonder to Miss Nomer how casually this phrase is used in the sense of bring to a climax or reach a crisis. Give it more than a passing thought, and it must occur to you that the phrase is more than a trifle repulsive. After all, it is an infected pimple that is *brought to a head* when sufficient pus forms to push its way up through the surface of the skin. Once the pimple or boil or blemish is *brought to a head*, its possessor can look forward to the moment of its eruption into a running sore. Some fun!

Not only is *bring to a head* distasteful, it is also a cliché. Use "bring to a climax," "reach a crisis," or "precipitate" instead.

broadcast / broadcasted   -2 VOQ

Some authorities insist that *broadcast* is a present-tense verb only and that *broadcasted* is the correct form for the past and past participle. To Miss Nomer's practiced ear, *broadcasted* simply sounds wrong, and, on the model of its root, *cast*, she believes it should be treated as an irregular verb— that is, *broadcast* should serve for the present-tense as well as the past-tense form. Also see *telecast / telecasted*.

brute / beast

See *beast / brute*.

bullet   -2 VOQ

Alas, this word is misused less of late than in the past. One frequently hears civilians refer quite professionally to *rounds* rather than *bullets*, and when the intended meaning is a unit of ammunition, *round* is, indeed, correct. The *bullet* is nothing more than the lead projectile mounted on top of the explosive *cartridge*. Thus one does not load a weapon with *bullets*, but with *cartridges* or *rounds*.

bullion / bouillon   -4 VOQ

Bullion and *bouillon* share the same Old French root, namely *boulir*, to bubble or boil, but the modern English word *bul-*

lion most commonly refers to ingots of precious metal, such as gold or silver, whereas, in English, *bouillon* is a clear, thin broth, which may be made from chicken or beef. Why the common root for two very different words? Just as chicken or beef are boiled and rendered for *bouillon*, so gold or silver are melted to be cast into *bullion*.

burgeon -2 VOQ

This is a word that deserves better care than it has received. Its literal meaning is to bud or to sprout, but it is more frequently used—or, rather, misused—figuratively, in the sense of to expand or to grow prodigiously. By all means, use the word figuratively, but only when you wish to suggest a process analogous to sprouting or budding. ''The population of the boom town *burgeoned* from under 5,000 in 1848 to 50,000 by 1851'' shows proper use of the word. Consider, however, the following: ''The Atlanta area's population *burgeoned* from 3 million to 3.5 million in just five years.'' Certainly this is rapid growth, but it is not analogous to budding, since 3 million is already a large number and the population of metropolitan Atlanta has been growing for a long time.

burglar / robber / thief -3 VOQ

A *burglar* steals unattended or inadequately guarded property, usually taking it from a home or place of business. He does not attack people, nor does he forcibly take such items as wallets, watches, jewelry, or purses from the person of his victim. That is the province of the *robber,* who forcibly takes property from people or takes property from attended or guarded houses or places of business. A *thief* may be a *burglar* or a *robber* and, in general usage, may be any malefactor who (at least in the opinion of the writer or speaker) does not earn what he appropriates: "The faucet still leaks. That plumber is a *thief*."

burglary / robbery   -3 VOQ

Burglary is a crime against property, whereas *robbery* is a crime against a person or persons. See the preceding entry.

burgle / burglarize   -4 VOQ

Burgle is a back-formation from *burglary*, and, like most back formations, it is nonstandard English. Even though many words ending in *-ize* are clumsy and questionable, *burglarize* is the standard form here, and *burgle* should be rejected.

but however / but nevertheless   -4 VOQ

However and *nevertheless* indicate opposition or exception. They need no assistance in doing this; therefore, butt out with *but*.

C

cache / cachet   -4 VOQ

Cache is pronounced "cash"—not "cash-A"—and refers to a store (often a hidden store) of goods, money, supplies, food, ammunition, and so forth. The word may also denote the hiding place itself. *Cache* may be used as a verb: to *cache* is to store something or hide it away. Computer-literate folk will recognize *cache* as the name of an electronic storage buffer that increases the speed with which certain data may be accessed by the computer. *Cachet*, which does rhyme with "cash-A," may refer to an official seal or a commemorative design stamped on an envelope, but more often *cachet* is a figurative seal of approval—a snobbish mark of quality or distinction. *Cachet* often certifies authenticity: "That he once got falling-down drunk with Ernest Hemingway gave him *cachet* as a writer."

caesarian section / cesarean section / cesarian section
−2 VOQ

Of these three, *cesarean section* is the preferred spelling. It is true that this surgical procedure is named for Julius Caesar, who, according to legend, was delivered by *cesarean*, but the most widely accepted spelling of the procedure is modified. Despite the operation's origin in a proper noun, it is spelled without an initial capital, and drops the *ae* in favor of the simple *e*.

callous / callus
-3.5 VOQ

Miss Nomer has lost her patience with the legions who use *callous* as both noun ("I have a *callous* on my foot") and adjective ("You are a *callous* human being"). The noun is *callus*, a direct borrowing from the Latin original, whereas the adjective is *callous*. "Your indifference to the pain my *callus* inflicts is singularly *callous*."

can / may
-2 VOQ

Miss Nomer gives the misuse of this pair a moderately low VOQ because the correction of the error is usually far more obnoxious than the error itself. Youngster: "Can I ride my bicycle?" Parent: "I don't know. *Can* you?" Please. Enough already. *Can* refers to ability or capability, whereas *may* refers to permission. Literally, "*Can* I ride my bicycle?" means "Do I have the ability to ride my bicycle?" Of course, what is really intended here is "*May* I ride my bicycle?"— that is, "Do I have your permission to ride?"

cancel out   -3 VOQ

A common phrase—and quite redundant. *Cancel* has no need of *out*.

canon / cannon   -4 VOQ

If you are smart enough to have occasion to use the word *canon*, you are smart enough to spell it with only one *n*. *Canon* may mean an ecclesiastical law or a member of certain religious communities; the books of the Bible accepted as Holy Scripture; the works of a writer or composer that are accepted as authentic; the part of the Mass after the Preface and Sanctus and ending just prior to the Lord's Prayer; the calendar of saints of the Roman Catholic church; an established principle; a basis for judgment; or a musical composition or passage in which a melody is repeated by two or more voices overlapping in time and in the same or a related key. A *cannon*—with two *n*'s—is a mounted artillery piece that fires heavy missiles, such as cannonballs.

can't hardly   -5 VOQ

This is an illiteracy, plain and simple. Avoid it. The correct phrase is *can hardly,* as in "I *can hardly* hear you."

can't seem   -1.5 VOQ

"He just *can't seem* to make up his mind." This is common usage, and many authorities accept it. But it has always bothered Miss Nomer, because the notion of *can't seem* is blatantly illogical, even nonsensical. Avoid it if possible.

capacity / ability

See *ability / capacity*.

capital / capitol   -3.5 VOQ

These two words are commonly confused. A government *capital* is a city or town, while a *capitol* is the government's chief building. For example, the state *capital* of Illinois is the town of Springfield, which includes a domed building in which the state legislature meets. This is the *capitol*. When referring to the home of the United States Congress, the *Capitol* is treated as a proper noun, and its first letter is—what else?—capitalized.

carat / caret / carrot / karat   -3.5 VOQ

Only one item in this bunch would interest a rabbit—*carrot*. The rest appeal to different audiences. *Carat* is a unit of weight for precious stones. *Karat* is a unit of measure for the fineness of gold, with each unit equal to $\frac{1}{24}$ of the whole—in other words, pure gold is 24-*karat*. Some authorities consider these variant spellings of the same word; *carat* is almost always applied to stones, however, and *karat* to gold. Note, too, that those who are knowledgeable about gems and gold use the terms without a plural *s*: "This gold is 12-*karat* (not *karats*).

Now this leaves us with the humble *caret*, which is what you call the little wedge that writers, editors, and proofreaders use to indicate that something is to be inserted: ∧ (The *caret* looks a lot like an inverted *V*). The humble word traces its lineage to ancient Rome, where it was the third person singular present tense of *carere*, "to lack." In other words, a *caret* says "Something is lacking."

careen   -1 VOQ

Careen is often used as a more colorful synonym for the verb *speed*: "The car *careened* down the street," as most people would see it, means the same as "The car *sped* down the street." But, to be precise, *careen* means to tilt or to heel over. It is derived from nautical usage; ships were often *careened,* or tilted over in dry dock to enable repairs to be made to the hull. Thus a *careening* car is traveling at such high speed that it actually tilts, maybe even gliding on two wheels.

catalog / catalogue   -1 VOQ

Nowadays, in the United States, the trend is toward simplifying this word. But see *dialog / dialogue*.

caustic / costive   -2 VOQ

Caustic means corrosive or capable of burning, and it is often used figuratively as an adjective to describe a particularly scorching satire. Note, however, that *caustic* substances are hydroxides of light metals and are therefore alkaline, like lye (*caustic* soda, or sodium hydroxide); therefore, an "*acid* remark" cannot properly be called *caustic*, even though it burns.

It is far worse, of course, to confuse *caustic* with *costive*, which denotes the condition of suffering from constipation. By metaphoric extension, to be *costive* is also to be slow or sluggish or even stingy.

cede / secede -4 VOQ

Both of these words are rooted in the Latin *cedere*, "to go," but *cede* means to yield possession of something (usually land) to another person, entity, or nation, usually by formal treaty, while *secede* (which adds the Latin prefix *se-*, signifying "apart") means to withdraw from membership in an organization or alliance. "In 1791, Virginia and Maryland *ceded* land to the federal government for the District of Columbia, but in 1861, Virginia *seceded* from the United States."

celebrant -3 VOQ

This is *not* a word that should be used to describe one who attends a party. It's meaning is considerably more solemn. A *celebrant* is a participant in a religious ceremony: "The priest is the principal *celebrant* of the Mass." Partygoers are *celebrators*, *revelers*, *merrymakers*, or *guests*.

center around -3 VOQ

Miss Nomer is acquainted with many people who find this phrase especially irritating. As a verb, *center* means to gather to a point; therefore, *center around* is without sense. Use *center in*, *center on*, or *center at* instead of *center around*: "The controversy *centered on* five points." "The trouble was *centered at* High Street and Western."

ceremonial / ceremonious   -3 VOQ

Be careful with these. *Ceremonial* describes something that is used in a ceremony or an event that is like a ceremony: "The emperor wore a *ceremonial* sword at all *ceremonial* occasions." *Ceremonious* should be applied not to things or events, but to attitude, manner, gestures, or actions. It may also be used to describe a person who has a *ceremonious* attitude or indulges in *ceremonious* actions. "The usher indicated our seats with a *ceremonious* flourish of his hand."

character / reputation   -2 VOQ

Character and *reputation* are intimately related aspects of a person, but distinct words. *Character* refers to the moral and ethical qualities of an individual. *Reputation* is a matter of perception; it is the public's or community's estimation of a person. Compare this—"Joe is fair-minded and scrupulously honest, a person of spotless *character*"—to this: "Everyone believes Joe is fair-minded and scrupulously honest; his *reputation* is spotless." *Character* applies chiefly to a person, while reputation can be applied to a thing: "In its day, the Packard had a great *reputation* as a solid luxury automobile." Note that *character* can be applied figuratively to a thing, in effect comparing the thing to a person: "That old rocking chair has real *character*."

children's / childrens'   -4 VOQ

Take care! It's easy to make careless mistakes with this irregular plural. *Children's* is the correct plural possessive, and *childrens'* is wrong.

chockful / chock-full   -2 VOQ

The preferred spelling is two words, hyphenated.

chutzpa / chutzpah / hutspah / hutzpa   -2 VOQ

You may find partisans for each of these spellings, but the most widely accepted by far is *chutzpah*. Use it.

claim   -1 VOQ

As a verb, *claim* should be used in the sense of *assert* or *declare* only in asserting or declaring a right, entitlement, or ownership: "Columbus *claimed* the New World for Isabella and Ferdinand of Spain." It should not be generally and indiscriminately used in the place of *assert*, *declare,* or other words of similar meaning: "Even as the police officer handed him the ticket, Jack continued to *claim* that the traffic light had malfunctioned." *Declare* or *protest* would be better choices here. Although the careless use of *claim* is common, it is no great crime. Avoid it if you can, but if you commit the error, it will either pass unnoticed or be forgiven.

classic / classical   -2.5 VOQ

There are three problems here. First, *classic* and *classical* may not be used interchangeably. *Classic* signifies the best, a work of art, a piece of music, a theatrical performance, or some other human creation that is destined to endure and draw wide admiration. *Classical* pertains primarily to the world, times, and culture of the Greeks and Romans in their heyday. It may also be used to describe analogous historical high periods in other cultures—for example, "the *classical* period of Mayan civilization"—and, even more generally, it may be used to describe other generally acknowledged, well-established periods or systems of the past, as in "*classical* Freudian psychology versus the innovations of Erik Erikson" or "*classical* music versus pop."

A second problem is that *classic* should not be used as a synonym for *typical or archetypal*. Statements such as "He was a *classic* idiot" would represent a humorous use of *classic*—and would therefore be acceptable—if they weren't so thoroughly overused. Avoid such use.

That brings us to the third problem. *Classic* has become a cliché. It is used to describe everything from errors committed on the baseball diamond to the taste of the hot dogs served in the stands. Reserve and conserve this word.

clench / clinch   -3 VOQ

Clench and *clinch* both mean grasp or fasten, but *clench* is the word generally used when physical grasping or fastening is the intended meaning: "John *clenched* his fist." *Clinch* is the choice when figurative grasping or fastening is intended: "That last goal *clinched* the victory." In one special case, *clinch* applies to a physical situation: a passionate embrace, especially between two actors on the silver screen—"The Bogart and Bacall characters spoke lovingly to each other, then came the *clinch*."

climactic / climatic   -3 VOQ

It's easy to stumble over this pair. *Climatic* refers to *climate*, whereas *climactic* means most intense, the point of climax in a drama, narrative, or historical process or series of events: "The *climactic* moment of the play comes when Lear discovers that two of his daughters have betrayed him."

climax -4 VOQ

Climax does not mean end or conclusion, although it is often mistakenly used in this sense. It is the point of greatest intensity, often the turning point, in a drama, narrative, or historical process or series of events. The structure of classical drama builds, in the manner of a crescendo, to the *climax*, then falls away from that point to the resolution, which is the end of the play. Typically, there is a good deal of story left after the *climax* has been reached.

close proximity -4 VOQ

Proximity means closeness; therefore, *close proximity* is redundant and strikes most careful readers or listeners as particularly stupid.

closure / cloture -3 VOQ

Closure is the act of closing, bringing to an end, or bringing to a conclusion. In the last-mentioned sense, *closure* implies a degree of satisfaction or emotional relief: "The conviction of the murderer brought a feeling of *closure* to the victim's family." Far more specialized is *cloture* (pronounced "klochur"), which denotes the practice of closing debate—in the British House of Commons (where the term originated in 1882) or in the U.S. Congress—by putting the matter to a vote.

coffee klatch / coffee klatsch -2 VOQ

The preferred spelling is *klatch*. To those who object, pointing out that the German word is *Klatsch*, so why drop the *s*? you may respond that the German word is actually *Kaffeeklatsch*, and that if we Anglicize *Kaffee*, why not *klatsch*?

cohort   -4 VOQ

Cohort is commonly shanghaied and pressed into involuntary servitude as a synonym for *comrade, ally, colleague, fellow conspirator, fellow member*, and the like. The mistake here is the assumption that *co-* is used as a prefix, as in *copilot, costar, coconspirator,* or *coauthor*. But *cohort* has no prefix; the word comes from a Latin original signifying a military unit, specifically a Roman Legion unit of three hundred to six hundred men. Its proper modern English-language use is as a synonym for *company, group*, or *band*, as in "a *cohort* of children swept through the playground." The word also has a specialized meaning as a generational group defined in demographical, statistical, or market research: "The *cohort* of consumers aged twenty-three to twenty-six was more likely to buy the product than the *cohort* aged twenty-seven to thirty-three."

collectables / collectibles   -3 VOQ

If it's not exactly junk but it's no museum piece either, chances are it's a *collectible*. The only acceptable spelling is with an *i*, not an *a*.

collide   -2 VOQ

An automobile can crash into a tree, but it cannot *collide* with a tree—unless, by some freak of nature, the tree is in motion. All of the entities involved in a *collision* must be in motion. Otherwise, the event is a crash.

commode   **-1 VOQ**

A *commode* is a low cabinet or chest of drawers. It may also refer to a kind of portable vanity-and-washstand combination, often mounted on wheels. While *commode* can be used as synonym for toilet, this tends to be perceived as a lame attempt at euphemism. Best to use *toilet* for toilet.

common / mutual   **-1.5 VOQ**

In addition to meaning widespread, prevalent, ordinary, and usual, *common* may also mean joint—that is, belonging to or shared by two or more people, things, or entities: "The house is our *common* property." *Mutual* describes a reciprocal relationship between two or more things or people— for example, "their *mutual* respect" is the equivalent of "their respect for each other." However, many people use *mutual* as a synonym for *common*, as in "our *mutual* interests." Sticklers correctly object to this as a misuse of *mutual*, but the practice is very, uh, *common*. Do note, however, that *mutual* can never be substituted for *common* in the sense of "general." In the Preamble to the U.S. Constitution, Thomas Jefferson was quite correct to write of promoting the "general welfare" and providing for the "*common* defense" rather than the "*mutual* welfare" and the "*mutual* defense."

compare to / compare with   **-3 VOQ**

The choice of preposition to follow *compare* is not a matter of arbitrary taste. *Compare to* is used to liken two things or to place two things in the same category: "F. Scott Fitzgerald *compared* the career of Dick Diver, the hero of *Tender Is the Night*, *to* the flight of a rocket, which is what he first thought of calling the novel." *Compare with* is used to evaluate two things side by side: "The performance of a $9,000 Geo cannot *compare with* the performance of an $80,000 Mercedes."

compendium   -4 VOQ

Commonly understood to denote a hefty tome, encyclopedic in scope, or, in fact, any vast, all-inclusive assemblage, a *compendium* is actually a brief summary or thorough outline.

complacent / complaisant / compliant   -3 VOQ

Complacent may mean self-satisfied and therefore unconcerned about much of anything. The word may also mean eager to please or amiable—which is precisely the meaning of *complaisant*. *Complaisant*, however, cannot be used in the sense of self-satisfied. Then there is *compliant*, which means obedient, obliging, yielding; it usually connotes submissiveness.

complement / compliment   -3 VOQ

A vowel makes all the difference. *Complement*, which may be used as a noun or a verb, pertains to completeness or to supplementing something: "Sir, the platoon's full *complement* is present, Sir!" Or "This scarf will *complement* your lovely blouse very nicely." *Compliment*, also usable as a noun or a verb, pertains to praise and courtesy: "Sergeant, you are very thorough. I hope you will accept that as a *compliment*." Or "I want to *compliment* you on your choice of scarf."

complete / replete   -3 VOQ

Complete means entire, whole, or finished. *Replete* means
full or possessing in abundance. Use *with* with *replete*.

compose / comprise   -3.5 VOQ

The confusion between *compose* and *comprise* is the peeve
of many a guardian of the language. To *compose* is to as-
semble or create, whereas to *comprise* is to contain, to include, or to encompass. Just remember this: The whole
comprises the parts; the parts *compose* the whole. "Water
comprises hydrogen and oxygen—that is, hydrogen and oxygen *compose* water."

comprehend / apprehend

See *apprehend / comprehend*.

compulsory / mandatory   -2 VOQ

These are almost synonymous, in that both mean required;
however, *compulsory* is stronger than *mandatory* because it
carries the implication of enforcement and penalty for failure
to comply with whatever is required.

concern   -2 VOQ

It is appropriate to speak of a business *concern* as synonymous with a business organization, but it is not acceptable
to use the term to describe a professional organization: "The
doctor is associated with a large medical *concern*." The appropriate term here is *practice*.

conclave / enclave -3 VOQ

Let's tackle *conclave* first. Properly used, it describes a meeting behind closed doors or a secret meeting. It is, therefore, a mistake to use it as a synonym for *convention,* which is hardly a secret meeting: "Joe drank too much at the traveling salesmen's *conclave.*" Moreover, the word is often confused with *enclave,* which is not a meeting at all, secret or public, but a distinctly bounded area within a larger area, such as a country or part of a country wholly surrounded by the territory of another nation, or an ethnically homogenous neighborhood within an ethnically diverse city.

confute / refute -2 VOQ

These are nearly synonymous, but *confute* is stronger. It means to disprove a statement, assertion, or proposition absolutely. *Refute* means to supply evidence against a statement, assertion, or proposition. Also see *rebut / refute.*

connive -4 VOQ

Connive is one of a select group of words that are misused far more often than they are used correctly. Most writers and speakers would not hesitate to tell you that the word is a synonym for *conspire, wheedle, act underhandedly,* or *contrive.* In truth, *connive* means nothing of the kind. Derived from a Latin word meaning to wink, it denotes the act of shutting one's eyes to a wrongdoing, an irregularity, or some other disagreeable occurrence: "The company's controller habitually *connived at* irregularities in the corporate books."

connote / denote -3 VOQ

The distinction between these is sharp and easily expressed. To *connote* is to imply or suggest. To *denote* is simply to mean. "The word 'obesity' *denotes* the state of being overweight, but, for many people, it *connotes* laziness, gluttony, and sluggishness."

consensus of opinion -3.5 VOQ

Redundant, wasteful, annoying. *Consensus* means general agreement and effectively carries the sense of *opinion* with it. There is no reason to tack on two extra words.

contagious / infectious -2 VOQ

The difference between these words is subtle, unless you happen to be in the vicinity of a person with a deadly disease. A sickness is *contagious* if it is communicable by mere contact with or proximity to an infected person or thing. Colds and the flu are good examples of *contagious* diseases. An *infectious* disease is transmitted by a specific kind of contact. Sexually transmitted diseases are more properly spoken of as *infectious* rather than *contagious*.

contemporary / contemporaneous -4 VOQ

Albert Einstein convinced the world (at least he succeeded in convincing Miss Nomer) that reality is a matter of relativity. *Contemporary* does not necessarily mean *modern*. Instead, think of the word in its root sense of "existing at the same time." Then consider that context determines meaning. "Thomas Jefferson was a *contemporary* of John Adams," but of course neither man is *contemporary* in the sense of being alive today. If, for example, you are writing an essay on eighteenth-century America, the use of *contemporary* should probably be restricted to events within the eighteenth-century arena, and *modern* could be used for comparisons with events in the present day. In the absence of a historical context, however, *contemporary* may be safely used as a synonym for *current, present-day,* or *modern.* Note, however, that while the meaning of *contemporary* is relative to context, the word itself is an absolute rather than a matter of degree. You cannot use *more* or *less* to modify *contemporary.*

Contemporaneous means happening or existing during the same period of time: "The Wright Brothers and Marconi were *contemporaries*, and the airplane and the radio were *contemporaneous* inventions."

## contemptible / contemptuous	-3.5 VOQ

Similar in sound, these two words occupy opposing sides of the fence. A *contemptible* thing, statement, idea, or person deserves contempt. A *contemptuous* person has contempt for some things, ideas, or people. A person can be generally *contemptuous* or can be *contemptuous of* some particular thing, person, or idea: "Partisans of the composer Richard Wagner were *contemptuous of* traditional music, such as that of Brahms."

## continual / continuous	-3 VOQ

Miss Nomer finds the careless misuse of these two words highly annoying. *Continual* applies to close and prolonged recurrence, whereas *continuous* pertains to an uninterrupted flow or a spatial extension. "I've had a *continuous* stream of work cross my desk today, even while I suffered from *continual* interruptions. Fortunately, I managed to save some time, because the rest room and the coffee-break room are in a hallway that is conveniently *continuous* with my office.''

contrary / opposite   -4 VOQ

It will come as a shock to some that these two words are not synonymous and interchangeable. Indeed, they have significantly different logical functions. Consider this statement: ''All barking dogs bite.'' Here is the *contrary* of this statement: ''Not all barking dogs bite.'' And here is the *opposite*: ''No barking dogs bite.'' The *contrary* statement actually includes, to a degree, both the positive statement and the *opposite* statement.

converse / reverse   -4 VOQ

As *contrary* and *opposite* are not synonymous, neither are *converse* and *reverse*. Consider again: ''All barking dogs bite.'' The *converse* is ''All biting dogs bark.'' The *converse* of a statement transposes the principal elements of the statement. *Reverse* is the most general word you can use to express oppositeness. It can subsume *converse* (but, *conversely*, *converse* cannot subsume it), and, for that matter, it can also subsume *contrary* and *opposite*. The statement ''All barking dogs bite, and the *reverse* is also true'' could mean any, some, or all of the following: ''Not all barking dogs bite,'' ''No barking dogs bite,'' and ''All biting dogs bark.''

convince / persuade   -2 VOQ

The difference between these two is a matter of degree. To *convince* is to bring someone to a course of action or a firm belief by use of compelling argument or evidence. To *per-*

suade is to do the same by the use of argument, logical reasoning, or emotional entreaty. *Convince* implies a greater degree of certainty than *persuade*.

couch / davenport / divan / sofa   -1 VOQ

You may well go through life using these words interchangeably without ill effect. Be aware, however, that some people consider *sofa* in all cases preferable to *couch*, which strikes particularly sensitive ears as vaguely vulgar. One seldom hears *davenport* anymore. In the strictest sense, it describes a particularly large *sofa*. *Divan* is not heard very frequently, either. It is a long, backless *sofa*, usually placed against a wall and piled with pillows.

could care less   -4 VOQ

The universe holds many mysteries, among the least of which is how the expression "I couldn't care less" became translated into the manifestly nonsensical "I *could care less*." What's the point here? If you *could* care less about a particular issue, then that issue must have some importance as far as you are concerned. If you could *not* care less, then the issue has no importance to you.

could of   -5 VOQ

The right word is *could've*—a contraction of *could have*—as in, "I *could've* been a contender." *Could of* is a severe illiteracy and must be avoided.

council / counsel
-3.5 VOQ

A *council* is an authoritative board, an assembly convened for discussion, consultation, or deliberation. It is always a noun. *Counsel* may be a noun or a verb. As a noun, it means advice or guidance, with the implication that the advice or guidance comes from a trusted or respected person. The word may also mean a private or guarded opinion: "I will keep my own *counsel* on this matter." Used as a verb, to *counsel* is to advise. Often, the implication is that the advice is therapeutic, sensitive, and healing.

counsel / counselor / attorney / lawyer

See *attorney / lawyer / counsel / counselor*.

country / nation
-2 VOQ

Use *nation* when you wish to denote the people of a country, and *country* when you want to emphasize territory: "the people of this *nation*," "the rivers in our *country*."

craft
-2 VOQ

When used in place of *boat, airplane*, or *space vehicle*, the plural of *craft* is *craft*, not *crafts*.

crass
-3 VOQ

The phrase "*crass* commercialism" is a cliché. Although it is very commonly used, it does not mean what its users intend it to mean. Primarily, *crass* means stupid, bluntly stupid, obtuse. Oddly, it is rarely used in this sense. Instead, phrases like "*crass* commercialism" lean on the word's distantly secondary meaning—coarse, gross, and insensitive. Either everyone must get together and decide formally to shift the primary meaning of this word, or everyone should use it with greater respect for its more important meaning.

credence / credibility / credulity   -3 VOQ

All of these have to do with trust and belief. *Credence* may be taken as a synonym for precisely these two words. Note, however, that while you may *trust* or *believe* someone, *credence* is something you *give*: "I don't *give* much *credence* to anything Nancy says." *Credibility* is a capacity to induce belief. A person, an interpretation, or a statement may be *credible* or may have *credibility*. "Nancy's *credibility* is in serious doubt." *Credulity* is an exaggerated tendency to believe—in a word, gullibility: "I don't have the *credulity* to believe everything Nancy tells me. I am just not that *credulous*."

crescendo   -3 VOQ

In music, a *crescendo* is a progressive, even increase in loudness. The term may be borrowed for analogy in other contexts—for example, "As news of the court's decision spreads, officials anticipate a *crescendo* of public complaint." *Crescendo* denotes a process, not a level, a point, a plateau, or a moment. "As news of the court's decision spread, public complaint reached a new *crescendo*" is nonsense. Substitute *level, height, intensity,* or some other word denoting a point or degree.

crippled -4 VOQ

In most contexts, this word is offensive or, at the very least, insensitive. You may use *physically challenged*, but if that phrase seems too politically correct to you, simply say ''person with a disability.'' You should also avoid *disabled* and *handicapped*.

criteria -3.5 VOQ

Criteria is the plural form of *criterion*. If you have reference to more than one specification or requirement, by all means use *criteria*, but if you intend a single specification or requirement, *criterion* is the only acceptable word.

cue / que / queue -1.5 VOQ

Cue is often misspelled *que*. That's the first problem. The word means a signal, hint, suggestion; in music and in some other performing arts, a *cue* is a reminder or a prompt to make an entrance or perform some action; in psychology, *cue* may be used synonymously with *stimulus*. To devotees of pool, billiards, or snooker, a *cue* is the tapered leather-tipped rod used to send the *cue* ball on its way into the numbered balls. *Cue* may also function as a verb, meaning to give a cue, a hint, a signal: ''Just *cue* me when you're ready to go.''

A *queue* is a line of waiting people, vehicles, or—in computer science—bits of data (waiting their turn to be processed). *Queue* may function as a verb, almost always with the addition of the auxiliary *up*: ''Please *queue* up, ladies and gentlemen, and wait your turn to be served.'' A *queue* is also a long braid of hair, a pigtail, especially as worn by many Chinese men prior to the revolutions of the twentieth century. While some authorities accept *cue* as a variant spelling of *queue*, you'll be on much safer ground if you keep the spellings and words distinct.

culminate   -3 VOQ

It will come as a surprise to the barbaric hordes who routinely misuse this word that *culminate* does not signify conclusion, ending, result, or outcome, but means "to reach the highest point." It is therefore incorrect to say "The process of sorting the mail *culminates* in delivery," since this mundane chain of events hardly ends in a high point. (Use *ends* instead.) It is appropriate, however, to use the word in the following: "Beethoven's symphonic production *culminated* in the monumental Ninth Symphony." Certainly the last of Beethoven's symphonies is a high point in his career and in the history of Western music. If you believed that the *Fifth*, rather than the *Ninth Symphony*, is the high point of Beethoven's symphonic output, you would still be correct in writing this sentence, substituting *Fifth* for *Ninth*, even though Beethoven wrote four more symphonies after the *Fifth*. (Musicologists could argue with you, but not grammarians.)

Note that *culminate* must take a preposition, *in,* and cannot stand alone. "The Ninth Symphony *culminated* Beethoven's symphonic output" lacks the preposition and is therefore an incorrect use of the verb.

D

dastardly -2 VOQ

Few of us use this word anymore, but most of us believe it is a melodramatic synonym for *evil*, *vicious*, and *contemptible*. It is not. A *dastardly* act or a *dastardly* villain is a deed or person tinged with the lowest form of cowardice. When President Franklin Delano Roosevelt, in requesting of Congress a declaration of war against Japan following the December 7, 1941, attack on Pearl Harbor, called the attack *dastardly*, he meant that it was cowardly—an unprovoked sneak attack—not vicious.

data -1 VOQ

Sticklers for staying true to Latin roots point out that *data* is the plural of *datum* and should therefore always be treated as a plural: "The *data* prove" rather than "The *data* proves." Yet in general usage, treating *data* as a plural strikes the ear as odd or just plain wrong. Miss Nomer favors the ear and advises you to use *data* with a singular verb.

One more word of advice, however. Don't use *data* when *information* is more appropriate. *Data* should be reserved for factual information that is being subjected to analysis. Of course, *data* also denotes the results of scientific experiments and information that is represented in a form suitable for processing by a computer.

davenport / couch / divan / sofa

See *couch / davenport / divan / sofa*.

deadly / deathly   -3 VOQ

Deadly things can kill you, but *deathly* things merely remind you of death: "As soon as Michael saw the *deadly* coral snake in his tent, he turned *deathly* pale."

deaf   -2 VOQ

Many hearing-impaired persons do not object to the term *deaf*; however, "hearing impaired" or "person with a hearing impairment" is preferable.

deaf and dumb   -5 VOQ

This phrase is offensive and entirely inappropriate. Never use it. Use such phrases as "hearing and speech impaired" or "a person with hearing and speech difficulties."

deaf mute   -5 VOQ

This is an outmoded, dehumanizing, and offensive term. Again, use such phrases as "hearing and speech impaired" or a "person with hearing and speech difficulties" instead.

debut / premiere   -2 VOQ

The first public appearance of a performer, an artist, or a musician is a *debut*. The first public performance of a play, a work of music, a show, a movie, and so on is a *premiere*. Both of these words are often used as verbs: "The young violinist *debuted* to great acclaim as she *premiered* the concerto she had composed.'' Also see *premier / premiere*.

decimate   -2 VOQ

If one were a literal-minded prig, which Miss Nomer is not, one would insist that *decimate* be used only to describe those situations in which one-tenth of something (usually an army) was destroyed. That is the literal meaning of *decimate*. However, it is perfectly acceptable to extend the meaning of *decimate* to denote any case of significant destruction. Be aware, however, that the word is not synonymous with *obliterate* or *annihilate*, which signify total destruction, and it cannot be preceded by such adverbs as *completely* or *totally*, since *decimate* refers to partial destruction.

decry / descry   -4 VOQ

To *decry* is to denounce, which is very different from *descry*, a word that means to see, make out, discern, or recognize. *Descry* is more than faintly archaic and is rarely encountered in modern writing.

deduce / adduce / induce   -4 VOQ

To *deduce* or *induce* is to conclude or infer. In the case of *deduction*, the conclusions relate to particular things and are based on general principles: Dogs have four legs (general principle). Ajax is a dog (particular thing). Ajax has four legs (conclusion about the particular thing based on a general principle). *Induction* examines a particular thing or things to reach a conclusion concerning a general principle or principles: The dogs Ajax, Achilles, and Hector have four legs (particular things). Therefore, all dogs have four legs (general

principle inferred). *Adduce* is the odd word out in this group.
It means to use as an example or offer for consideration: To
support his conclusion that all dogs have four legs, Bill *ad-
duced* Ajax, Achilles, and Hector.

deductive / inductive

See *deduce*.

defective / deficient   -3.5 VOQ

Both of these words describe undesirable conditions, but they
differ significantly. A *defective* product is flawed, having
been incorrectly manufactured; *defective* reasoning is also
flawed, often because of mistaken assumptions or inaccurate
data. A *deficient* product is not incorrectly manufactured but
poorly manufactured, perhaps using cheap materials; similarly, *deficient* reasoning may proceed from correct assumptions and adequate data but fail to take into account all of
the possibilities, or it may draw hasty conclusions or lack
creativity. The concept of *defective* concerns flaw, whereas
the concept of *deficient* concerns lack of quality.

definite / definitive   -3 VOQ

Definite pertains to the quality of exact and absolute delim-
itation. *Definitive* is applied to something—often a declaration—that is final and beyond argument. "The deadline by
which I must have your *definitive* decision is *definite*: two
o'clock on Thursday and no later. I can wait no longer."

deliberate / premeditated   -3 VOQ

A *deliberate* act is performed not impulsively but with full consciousness of one's actions. A *premeditated* act is one that has been planned in advance. Note that *deliberate* may also mean *purposeful*, and *deliberately* may mean *on purpose*.

delusion / illusion

See *illusion / delusion*.

denote / connote

See *connote / denote*.

deplore / abhor

See *abhor / deplore*.

deprecate / depreciate   -3 VOQ

Deprecate is very often misused in place of *depreciate*. To *deprecate* is to disapprove of: ''The principal *deprecated* the quality of the homework produced by the fifth graders.'' To *depreciate* is to devalue: '' 'My students work hard,' the fifth grade teacher said to the principal. 'Please don't *depreciate* them.' '' This is the proper use of *depreciate,* but note that many people would use *deprecate* here. This would be incorrect.

develope   -4 VOQ

A common—and particularly irritating—misspelling of develop. Remember what *potatoe* did to Dan Quayle? Remember Dan Quayle?

dexterous / dextrous   -2 VOQ

While *dextrous*, with two sleek syllables, seems more appropriate to what the word *dexterous* means (especially skilled or adept), the three-syllable version is favored.

diagnose   -2.5 VOQ

"Dr. Darwin *diagnosed* the patient as having acute laryngitis." Wrong. Dr. Darwin may or may not have been correct in diagnosing laryngitis (Miss Nomer makes no claim to medical expertise), but physicians *diagnose* medical conditions; they do not *diagnose* people. "Dr. Darwin *diagnosed* the patient's ailment as laryngitis," or "Dr. Darwin *diagnosed* laryngitis."

diagnosis / prognosis   -4 VOQ

Diagnosis is a determination of the nature of a disease or the cause or causes of a disorder. *Prognosis* is a forecast of the probable course and outcome of a disease or disorder. Note that both words may be applied, by analogy, to nonmedical problems and disorders, as in "The mechanic *diagnosed* a problem with my car's engine. Unfortunately, the *prognosis* he offered was not good. My car is about to die."

dialog / dialogue -2 VOQ

The preferred modern American spelling of *catalogue* is *catalog*, but *dialogue* remains *dialogue*. The simpler spelling has not found favor.

different -3 VOQ

Often, the commonest words are subject to the most abuse. *Different* is often used where there is no need for it. In "I saw him on two *different* occasions," for example, *different* is superfluous. If there were two occasions, they *had* to be *different*. Frequently, the use of *different* gives rise to errors in number: "Mr. Nixon used a quite *different* vocabulary inside the White House and in public." This should be "Mr. Nixon used quite *different* vocabularies inside the White House and in public." Better yet: "Mr. Nixon's vocabulary in the White House was quite *different* from the words he used in public."

And that brings us to another problem area. Is it *different from* or *different than*? About the correctness of *different from* there is no dispute. About *different than* there are reams of controversy. Ms. Nomer's advice: restrict yourself to *different from* to avoid any raised eyebrows, except before a dependant clause: "She is no different *than* you are."

Finally, there is the solo use of *different*: "I enjoy the music of R.E.M. It's *different*." This abuse of the word has prematurely aged generation upon generation of elementary school teachers. *"Different* from what?" they scream. *Different* cannot stand alone. It requires comparison.

differ from / differ with -4 VOQ

"I may *differ from* you, but I do not *differ with* you." To *differ from* is to be unlike, while to *differ with* is to disagree.

dilemma -3.5 VOQ

Clichés are usually best shunned, but here is a cliché that will help you use this word appropriately: "I found myself on the horns of a *dilemma*." Think about a bull or other horned animal. Horns on such animals always come in pairs, and that is precisely the way it is with *dilemmas*. They are always choices between two bad, unpleasant, or otherwise disagreeable alternatives. *Dilemma* is not a synonym for *problem, difficulty, quandary*, and the like, which do not necessarily denote being caught between a rock and a hard place—to use another cliché.

diphtheria -3 VOQ

The *phth* combination is almost as painful as this dread disease. Pronounce it "diftheria" rather than "dip-theria," and you will be more likely to spell the word correctly.

disabled -3 VOQ

Many believe that *disabled* is the polite and politically correct alternative to *crippled*. It is far preferable, however, to use "physically challenged" or simply to speak of a "person with a disability."

discomfiture / discomfort -3 VOQ

Discomfiture is not a fancier version of *discomfort*, despite the superficial similarity of the words. *Discomfort* is the absence of comfort, a condition ranging from mildly annoying to painful, whereas *discomfiture* is much more dire, signifying total, abject defeat.

discover / invent -4 VOQ

Most of us have no trouble with the concepts that make these words different. To *discover* a thing is to find or identify something already in existence but hitherto unknown or hidden. To *invent* a thing is to create something new, which did not exist before. Despite a grasp of this difference, *discover* is still frequently used in situations where *invent* belongs: "Marie and Pierre Curie *discovered* radium and *discovered* a process for extracting it from pitchblende." Here the first instance of *discovered* is correct, for radium is an element (atomic number 88) that exists in nature, but the second is wrong; they *invented* the process for extracting the element.

discreet / discrete -3.5 VOQ

These adjectives are frequently a source of confusion. To be *discreet* is to be prudent, circumspect, and careful not to reveal too much. The word *discrete* has a totally unrelated meaning, as separate, individual, or unconnected. "We have reached an agreement, which consists of three *discrete* parts. However, we must be *discreet* about publicizing the agreement prematurely." See *indiscreet / indiscrete*.

disinterested / uninterested -5 VOQ

If you want to enrage a person who cares about the language, misuse *disinterested* as a synonym for lacking interest. That's not what it means at all. To be *disinterested* is to be free from selfish or self-directed motives. A trial judge must be *disinterested* in the matters brought before his or her court. However, he or she must not be *uninterested* in them. *Uninterested* is the equivalent of lacking interest.

disown / disinherit   -3 VOQ

These two may very well be related in fact, but they are quite
distinct in meaning. To *disown* is to repudiate or renounce,
to refuse to acknowledge what is one's own. If you *disown*
your errant son, you sever him from yourself. You may take
another step and *disinherit* him, which means that you cut
him out of your last will and testament.

disregardless   -5 VOQ

This is an absurd illiteracy, the use of which makes one unfit
to walk among others of our species. The right word is *regardless*.

disremember   -5 VOQ

This word constitutes a criminal offense, although I *don't
remember* the number of the applicable statute.

dissect / bisect

See *bisect / dissect*.

divan / davenport / sofa / couch

See *couch / davenport / divan / sofa*.

dived / dove   -4 VOQ

The past tense of *dive* is *dived*, not *dove*. Many people refuse
to believe this. The clever among these will tell you that the
past tense of *drive* is *drove*; therefore, the past of *dive* must

be *dove*. You may skewer these deluded folk by asking (rhetorically, of course) if it follows, then, that the past participle *dive* is *diven*, since the past participle of *drive* is indisputably *driven*. In matters of grammar, it is advisable to take no prisoners.

dock / pier / wharf   -1.5 VOQ

Although the distinction between *dock*, on the one hand, and *pier* and *wharf*, on the other, is not nearly as consequential to seafaring folk as the difference between *boat* and *ship*, the misuse of any will brand the abuser as a landlubber. A *dock* is the space between two *piers* into which vessels enter. A *dock* may also exist without *piers*, as a cut into the shoreline, again for the use of boats or ships. A *pier* or *wharf* is the area used for the loading and unloading of cargo and passengers to and from the vessels in the *dock*. *Dock* is for craft; *pier* and *wharf* are for people and cargo.

doctor / physician   -1 VOQ

Nothing terrible will happen to you if you use these interchangeably; however, *doctor* most accurately refers to an academic degree, whereas *physician* refers to a member of the medical profession who holds the degree of doctor of medicine. *Physicians* call themselves *physicians* rather than *doctors*. Note that, while a surgeon is a *physician*, a distinction is sometimes made between the two; therefore, if you mean surgeon—a *physician* who performs surgical procedures— use *surgeon* rather than *physician*.

done   -2 VOQ

Done is properly used as the past participle of *do*, in expressions relating to what is socially acceptable ("In polite society, picking one's nose is just not *done*"), as a one-word expression signifying the consummation of a deal or bargain ("I'll offer you a 20 percent royalty." "*Done!*"), or to indicate that an item of food has been sufficiently cooked ("The turkey is *done*"). As a substitute for *finished* or *completed*, however, *done* strikes many writers, speakers, readers, and listeners as excessively informal and slangy: "Our work is *done*." Use *finished* or *completed* instead.

drank / drunk   -4 VOQ

The simple past and the past participle of *drink* cause more than their share of difficulty. *Drank* is the simple past: "I *drank* a glass of water. (Yes, water!)" *Drunk* is the past participle: "I *have drunk* many glasses of water in my time." *Drunk* cannot serve as the simple past, just as *drank* will not do as the past participle.

draperies / drapes   -2 VOQ

The same people who find *couch* a mildly rude word for *sofa* are likely to be put off by the use of *drapes* instead of *draperies* as a synonym for heavy curtains that "drape" in elegant folds. When in doubt about how to eat an unfamiliar food, use a knife and fork instead of your fingers. Similarly, prefer *draperies* to *drapes*.

draught / draft   -2 VOQ

Draught is not a fancy way to spell *draft*. It's the British way to spell *draft*, and it is not favored in American English.

drouth / drought -2 VOQ

In parts of the country and among people of a certain age, the *drouth* spelling of *drought* is common, as is pronouncing the *-th* at the end of the word. Both the spelling and the *-th* pronunciation are now considered nonstandard.

due to -2 VOQ

This phrase merits a -2 VOQ only because a significant number of people object to its being used in the sense of *because of*. The objectors argue that the phrase properly means *owed* or, in effect, *due*: "That money is *due to* me," which could also be expressed as "That money is *owed to* me" or "That money is *due* me." Indeed, controversy over the use of *due to* is at least as old as the early eighteenth century. Miss Nomer believes that *due to* is a legitimate alternative to "because of" or "owing to." However, if you wish to avoid controversy, use the latter two phrases rather than *due to*.

duffel bag / duffle bag / duffel coat / duffle coat -1 VOQ

So-called preferred spellings are often whimsical. Both *duffel* and *duffle* are acceptable, but, in the United States, one carries a *duffel bag* but wears a *duffle coat*. Actually, the term *duffle coat* is rarely heard on this side of the Atlantic—it denotes a hooded coat made of cheap woolen material—so the whimsy may forever escape our citizens.

dyeing / dying -2 VOQ

The gerund form of *die* is *dying*, but the gerund form of *dye* is *dyeing*, even though the combination of *e* and *-ing* looks peculiar.

E

each   -4 VOQ

The word causes inordinate confusion about the number of the verb related to it. In itself, *each* is singular; therefore, if it functions as the subject of a sentence, it takes a singular verb: "*Each* of you *is* responsible for *his* actions." Note also the singular pronoun, *his*.

Number agreement between *each* and subsequent nouns is a bit trickier. In a situation with a plural subject, if the verb comes before *each*, the subsequent noun is singular: "They are *each* eligible for *a prize*."

each other / one another   -1.5 VOQ, -3.5 VOQ

Traditionalists insist that *each other* be restricted to two objects, and *one another* be restricted to three or more: "Paul and Ann saw *each other* often. They had three or four friends in common, who visited *one another* on occasion." While this distinction is not strictly enforced, sticklers are always poised to pounce. Hence the -1.5 VOQ.

More serious—meriting a -3.5 VOQ—is the failure to secure number agreement when *each other* is used as a possessive pronoun. The following is wrong: "Ann and Paul visited *each other*'s house." Think of *each other's* as the grammatical equivalent of *their*. This being the case, you'll need a plural object: "Ann and Paul visited *each other's* houses."

eager / anxious

See *anxious / eager*.

effete   -4 VOQ

Effete looks as if it should be synonymous with *effeminate* and *foppish*. To coin a cliché, looks are deceiving. The word means exhausted, unfertile, worn out, jejune. When President Nixon's verbal hatchet man Spiro T. Agnew called the liberal media an ''effete corps of impudent snobs,'' he may well have meant that they were all used up and barren of ideas, but most people thought he was calling them a bunch of sissies.

egoist / egotist   -3 VOQ

The distinction between these two words is partly a question of nationality. Americans tend to use *egotist*, while Britons prefer *egoist*. But beyond this there *is* a difference in meaning between the two words. An *egotist* is a braggart who suffers from a greatly inflated view of his own importance. An *egoist* may or may not be boastful, but he is self-centered and selfish.

either   -4 VOQ

Either signifies one of two: *either* this or that. It should not be used with more than two choices: *either* this, that, or the other. *Either* takes singular objects: ''Have you shopped in *either* our Los Angeles or our Anaheim store?'' Don't use *stores*.

Linked with *or*, *either* can cause some difficulties. The *either . . . or* must be part of a parallel construction—that is, the two words must link two like grammatical elements, as in "Dad has *either* gone hunting *or* gone fishing." The elements on both sides of the *or* are grammatically similar and, therefore, parallel. Make the sentence a bit more economical by deleting the second "gone," and the structure is still sufficiently parallel. However, if you move the "either," you erode the parallelism: Dad *either* has gone hunting *or* fishing." If you attempt to restore the parallelism by repeating the entire phrase "has gone"—Dad *either* has gone hunting *or* has gone fishing"—you have a grammatically correct sentence, but an awkward and repetitious one. The idea is to keep the elements of an *either . . . or* sentence parallel, but with the minimum of words. Your meaning will be clearer, stronger.

elope   -3 VOQ

As *impeach* does not mean to eject from office but only to initiate proceedings with the object of removing an official from office, so *elope* does not mean to run off and get married. It means to run off with the intention of getting married. "The couple *eloped*" means that they ran off. Were they subsequently wed? Who knows? Better specify: "The couple *eloped* and were married in a Las Vegas chapel." See *impeach*.

else, other   -3 VOQ

Remember to include *else* or *other* in statements of comparatives: "Bill Gates has more money than anyone" is logically impossible, since the statement both includes and excludes Bill. Add *else* after *anyone*, and the statement makes sense. You could also express it with *other*: "Bill Gates has more money than any *other* person."

elude / allude

See *allude / elude*.

emend / amend

See *amend / emend*.

emigrant / immigrant / émigré   -2.5 VOQ

The first two words are, logically enough, parallel with the verb forms *emigrate / immigrate*: an *emigrant* is a person who *leaves* one country for another, while an *immigrant* is a new arrival in a country, having left his place of origin. (Because one is usually more concerned with the fact of having come to a new country than with the fact of having left the old, *immigrant* is more common than *emigrant*.) At least one usage of *emigrant* violates this neat, logical arrangement. The pioneers and homesteaders who trekked to the American West in the 1830s and throughout the nineteenth century were commonly called *emigrants*, regardless of national origin and without particular intent to emphasize that they were *leaving* rather than *arriving*. Finally, there is *émigré*, a person who has left his native country, almost always for political reasons. It is perfectly proper to speak of an *émigré from* or *to* a country. The connotation of *émigré* is of a more or less prominent person—typically an eminent figure who has suffered political persecution—whereas the connotation of *immigrant* is of one of the "masses," whose immigration was motivated by economic hardship or general oppression.

emigrate / immigrate   -2.5 VOQ

The prefix elements of these words make all the difference. *E-* is from a Latin root, signifying leaving, and *emigrate* therefore means to *leave* one country for another. *Im-* is also from the Latin, signifying entrance; *immigrate* means to *enter* one country from another. "Kelly *emigrated* from Ireland?" "That's right. He *immigrated* to the United States." What happens when both the country of origin and the country of choice are in the same sentence? Use the word that suits the thrust of the sentence: "Kelly *emigrated* from Ireland to the United States" puts the emphasis on the origin, whereas "Kelly *immigrated* to the United States from Ireland" puts the emphasis on the destination country. Take a look at *emigrant / immigrant / émigré*.

eminent / immanent / imminent   -4 VOQ

This trio of soundalikes poses grave hazards to the unwary. *Eminent* pertains to a prominent or outstanding person, as in "the *eminent* authority on the English language, Miss Nomer." *Immanent* is synonymous with inherent or indwelling: "Wisdom is *immanent* within Miss Nomer." (Secondarily, when used in a philosophical or theological context, the word may be a synonym for *subjective* and apply to something that exists entirely within the mind.) *Imminent* is synonymous with *impending*. Something *imminent* is something that is about to happen: "Now that you own this book, your total mastery of English usage is *imminent*."

emote -3 VOQ

Some words aren't so much wrong as just stupid. *Emote* is one of them. Linguists call it a back-formation, based on *emotion*. Better just to send it back where it came from. Use the phrase *express emotion* or *show feeling* instead.

empathy / sympathy -2 VOQ

Empathy is imagining oneself in the predicament or difficult situation of another. *Sympathy* is more simply a strong identification with the feelings of another person. *Empathy* requires a greater degree of imagination than *sympathy*.

enclave / conclave

See *conclave / enclave*.

endeavor / endeavour -2 VOQ

Although NASA christened one of its space shuttles *Endeavour*, most Americans favor the U.S. spelling, *endeavor*, rather than the British version.

end result -3.5 VOQ

A *result* is by definition an "end result." Eschew this redundant—and highly irritating—phrase.

enormity -4 VOQ

An elephant is an *enormous* animal, but it is not characterized by *enormity*, a word that has nothing whatever to do with size. *Enormity* denotes evil or wickedness; sometimes, it connotes outrageousness. The Nazis perpetrated war crimes on an enormous scale, but the *enormity* of their deeds has more to do with evil, than with vastness.

enquire / inquire / enquiry / inquiry -2 VOQ

While both spellings are acceptable, *inquire* and inquiry are preferred.

ensure / insure / assure

See *assure / ensure / insure*.

enthuse -1 VOQ

Even many traditionalists accept this verb in its intransitive form, but they still hold out against it in its transitive incarnation. As an intransitive verb, *enthuse* means to express enthusiasm, as in "She *enthused* over the vocal styling of Wayne Newton." As a transitive verb, *enthuse* means to make enthusiastic: "I'm afraid that Wayne Newton doesn't *enthuse* me." Be careful in stodgy company.

entitled -1 VOQ

This word is often used in sentences such as this: "The book is *entitled War and Peace*." It is better practice to use *titled* rather than *entitled* in such a context: "The book is *titled* War and Peace."

envelop / envelope -3 VOQ

Envelope is a noun meaning that flat paper package you stick a letter in for mailing. It rhymes with *cantaloupe* or *antelope*.

Envelop is a verb meaning to surround, to cover entirely, to hold. It rhymes with *develop*.

envy / jealousy -2 VOQ

These words are often used interchangeably without doing any *great* harm. Nevertheless, most authorities agree that *envy* denotes covetousness of someone else's possessions or advantages, whereas *jealousy* is a suspicious perception of rivalry. Think of the distinction this way: You may *envy* a person's money, power, and position in life, but you are *jealous* of the person himself.

epidemic / endemic / pandemic -2 VOQ

An *epidemic* is a more or less sudden outbreak of a disease within a defined population and area. A *pandemic* is an outbreak of a disease over a very vast area. "The outbreak of influenza following World War I was not an *epidemic* but a *pandemic,* which affected almost the entire world."

While *epidemic* and *pandemic* can be used as nouns as well as adjectives, *endemic* is an adjective only. It describes a disease or diseases that are more or less permanently associated with a particular population or geographical area: "Malaria is *endemic* to much of Ethiopia."

Before we leave this vale of tears, let's take another glance at *epidemic*. The word derives from two Greek originals, *epi*, a prefix meaning in or among, and *demos*, people: *among people*. Where does that leave animals? They're covered, at least partly. *Epizootic* is the adjective epidemiologists would use to describe a widespread outbreak among a defined animal population. There is no noun equivalent of *epidemic* for animals, however. One would use *epizootic disease* as the noun—that is, of course, if you can work up the nerve to use *such a word*.

epithet   -2 VOQ

Epithet is often used as a synonym for a disparaging or negative label attached to a person. It may even be used—misused—as a synonym for curse words and nasty names. In truth, the word is neither negative nor positive. It merely denotes an adjective or phrase that describes a characteristic or distinguishing quality of a person: Richard *the Lionhearted*, Ivan *the Terrible*, Otto *the Fat*, Simon *the Bold*, Aethelred *the Unready*, Edward *Longshanks*, Eric *the Red*, or, less exaltedly, *Diamond Jim* Brady (who was extravagent in dress), Admiral *Bull* Halsey (who was stubborn and aggressive), *Scarface* Al Capone (who bore a facial scar), and so on.

epitome

See *quintessence / essence / epitome*.

epoch / era   -2 VOQ

These are not synonyms. An *epoch* is a momentous turning point and, as such, signifies the beginning of an *era*, which is a span of time loosely defined by the pervasive influence of some event or chain of related events, a dominant personality, a dominant philosophy or religious belief, or even a dominant technology. It might be said, for example, that the *epoch* of the transistor launched us into the electronic *era*.

equal / more equal   -5 VOQ

Readers of George Orwell's *Animal Farm* will recall the political philosophy and slogan developed by the pigs who
came to rule as dictators over the other animals: "All animals
are equal, but some animals are more equal than others." As
political satire, this is appropriately devastating. As everyday
language, however, it is appalling. *Equal* is an absolute and
cannot be more or less. (Of course, you can imitate Orwell
and use *more equal* ironically: "I guess we're all created
equal, except in this organization some people are *more
equal* than others.")

equate   -4 VOQ

Equate means to make equal or express as equal. This is not
the same as deeming it a synonym for *equal*. *Equate* must
be followed by *with* or *to*: "We can't *equate* money *with*
virtue" is grammatically correct, whereas "Money does not
equate virtue" is grammatically wrong. *Equal* would work
well here.

esoteric / exoteric   -4 VOQ

No, *exoteric* is not a misprint for *esoteric*. It is a legitimate
word that means almost the opposite of *esoteric*. Whereas an
esoteric concept is difficult and unfamiliar to most people,
an *exoteric* one is known generally. "The rules of bridge are
esoteric, but those of blackjack are *exoteric*."

especial / special   -1 VOQ

There is a difference between these words, but it barely matters anymore. *Especial* means outstanding, whereas *special*

means particular (as opposed to general). *Special*, however, has come to assume both senses, and there is little we can do about it.

essence / epitome / quintessence

See *quintessence / essence / epitome*

esthetic / aesthetic

See *aesthetic / esthetic*.

estimation / opinion   -1.5 VOQ

"In my *estimation*, Madonna is not a great actress." The aesthetic validity of this declaration aside, *opinion* is more appropriate in this case than *estimation*, which describes a progress of quick, rough calculation.

etc. / and etc. / etc., etc.   -2 VOQ, -4 VOQ

Earning the sting of a -2 VOQ is the use of *etc.* in any context other than a technical or informal one. In most general narrative writing, "and so on" should be used instead of *etc.* Even worse is the use of *and* before *etc.* or the repetition of *etc.* as *etc., etc. Etc.* is an abbreviation for the Latin *et cetera*, which means "and other things of the same kind"; obviously, "and and other things of the same kind" is nonsense, as is repeating the phrase.

etymology / entomology   -4 VOQ

If you're smart enough to require either of these words, make certain you get them right. *Etymology* is the study of word history and origins. *Entomology* is the branch of biology devoted to the study of insects.

everyday / every day   -3.5 VOQ

Use *everyday* when you need an adjective—"my *everyday* clothes"—and *every day* when you need a noun: "I don't really wear my *everyday* clothes *every day*."

everyone / every one   -4 VOQ

Use *everyone* as a synonym for *everybody*, but *every one* when you mean *each*: "*Everyone* is welcome—that is, *every one* of you."

everyplace   -3 VOQ

Some authorities accept *everyplace* as a substitute for *everywhere*, but many more deem it too casual for inclusion in formal writing. Use *everywhere*, unless you wish to emphasize each place individually, in which case you may use *every place*: "I've put a name card at *every place*."

evoke / invoke   -3.5 VOQ

To *evoke* is to call up a memory or a feeling: "The slightest whiff of model airplane glue could *evoke* memories of his misspent childhood." To *invoke* is to call up a deity through supplication or prayer: "The Aztec priest *invoked* the name of the feathered serpent, Quetzlcoatl." *Invoke* may also be used in a secular context, to indicate, for example, an allusion to any revered person: "In an effort to bolster his sagging approval rating, the politician *invoked* the name of Abraham Lincoln."

exacerbate / exasperate   -3.5 VOQ

To *exacerbate* is to intensify in a negative way, or to make worse: "Don't *exacerbate* the situation by making snide comments." To *exasperate* is to frustrate, to vex, to make someone angry beyond words: "I warn you: don't *exasperate* me with your snide comments."

except / accept

See *accept / except*.

exceptionable / exceptional   -4 VOQ

Confusing these two is serious business. Something *exceptionable* provokes an exception—that is, disagreement and dispute—whereas something *exceptional* is extraordinary: "I find your *exceptional* lack of discretion *exceptionable*."

expire   -2 VOQ

This word is often used as a euphemism for *die*. Like most euphemisms, it succeeds only in making an unpleasant concept worse. Far better to say "he died" than "he *expired*."

explicit / implicit   -4 VOQ

These are mirror images of each other. An *explicit* statement is clear, specific, and straightforward. An *implicit* remark is suggested but not stated in so many words. *Implicit* can also be used to point out an unstated meaning within some text or discourse: "His respect for the mayor was *implicit* in his remarks."

expresso / espresso -2.5 VOQ

Many authorities accept *expresso* as an alternate spelling of *espresso,* but many others may condemn the *x* spelling. Follow the Italian original, and you cannot go wrong.

F

fabulous -3 VOQ

What it *really* means is fabled—that is, celebrated in fable and legend. By extension, the word may be applied to people, things, and events so extraordinary as to be beyond belief and therefore partaking of the world of fable. *Fabulous* is a lovely word that has been pressed into use to describe anything that is particularly agreeable, pleasant, nice, or good: "Sally bought a *fabulous* coat." It gets even worse: "Yes, it is *the most fabulous* coat I've ever seen." Beware of such linguistic inflation, which soon renders even the best of words valueless.

factious / factitious / fictitious / fractious -3.5 VOQ

These four make for a juicy utterance, full of fricatives and sibilants (*f* and *s* sounds). Let's sort them out. *Factious* ("fak-shus") means causing dissent, which is almost synonymous with *fractious* ("frak-shus"), though this word suggests that what is caused is more generally trouble than dissent. *Factitious* ("fak-tish-us") means made up or fabricated, often with the intention of deceiving or misleading. The word may also be applied to appearances that are deceptive or misleading: "His display of pleasure at our meeting was *factitious*." *Fictitious* is vaguely related to *factitious*, but means imaginary. Although something *fictitious* may be intended to deceive, no such deviousness is implied by the word. *Fictitious* may be taken as imaginary without any particular motive having been implied.

factor   -2 VOQ

This is a perfectly fine word, but it is typically worked to death. In addition to its specialized use in business, as an agent and, in an even narrower application, as a person who accepts accounts receivable as security for short-term loans; in mathematics, as one of two or more quantities that divide a given quantity without a remainder; and in physiology, as a substance with a specific biochemical function, such as blood-clotting factor, *factor* means something that contributes to a result or a process or an achievement. "John's great wealth was a significant *factor* in his success" is a fine use of the word. Careless writers and speakers, however, misuse *factor* as a synonym for such diverse words as *problem, thing, item,* and *fact*. Use the word sparingly and appropriately.

fact that, the   -1.5 VOQ

This common phrase is not wrong, but it is very often a waste of words and usually can be chucked: "He mentioned *the fact that* he was a Republican." Pare this down to *that*, or simply jump from "mentioned" to "he." At the beginning of a sentence, *That* should be used in place of *The fact that*: "*That* he had lied about having taken the money was never forgotten." In a minority of situations, *the fact that* is required: "I did not enjoy *the fact that* you were upset." In constructions with prepositions, *the fact that* is also needed: "I want to call your attention to *the fact that* Mr. Smith is not attending this meeting."

fail -3 VOQ

Fail implies an intention, objective, purpose, requirement, criterion, goal, or expectation that has not been achieved: "The expedition *failed* to reach the South Pole." *Fail* should be avoided when such intentionality is not implied. Consider this: "Peter *failed* to attend the meeting." Unless the speaker or writer knows that Peter intended or was required to attend the meeting, *did not* should be used instead of *failed to*.

farther / further -1.5 VOQ

For better or worse, most people use these interchangeably and have been doing so at least since the late Middle Ages; however, there is a difference between them. *Farther* is supposed to be used to indicate advancement over physical distance—"We traveled *farther* than they did"—while *further* should be reserved for advancement along a figurative or nonphysical dimension: "You can get *further* in your career if you work hard."

fault -2 VOQ

Fault is commonly used as a verb—"I can't *fault* him for that"—but many authorities frown on this, insisting that one can "find *fault*" but cannot simply *fault*. The safe course is to avoid using this word as a verb.

faze / phase   -3 VOQ

Faze is a verb, meaning to bother, disturb, or embarrass:
"Your antics don't *faze* me." *Phase* is usually a noun, meaning a step, aspect, or stage: "The first *phase* of the project
is planning." The word is sometimes also used as a verb in
the sense of changing something gradually or step by step.
In this case, it is used with *in* or *out*: "We will *phase in* the
new rules over the next month." Or: "We intend to *phase*
this product *out* by April."

feted / fetid / fated   -5 VOQ

The consequences of confounding *feted* with *fetid* could be
catastrophic. Confusing *feted* or *fetid* with *fated* would be
merely embarrassing. *Feted*—sometimes spelled with a circumflex accent (*fêted*)—may serve as the past tense of the
verb *fete* (pay honor to) or as an adjective meaning "hon-
ored": "On his return to the United States following victory
in Europe, General Eisenhower was *feted* (verb) lavishly. He
was a much-*feted* hero (adjective)." (*Fete* may also serve as
a noun, meaning party or celebration. *Fete* is borrowed from
the French *fête*, and French words with a circumflex accent
over a vowel often correspond to English words that have
an *s* following the vowel: *fête* is cognate with *fest* and *feast*,
just as, for example, *hôtel* is cognate with *hostel.*) Feted may
be correctly pronounced "fay-ted" or "fet-ed." The first
pronunciation runs the risk of confusion with *fated*, a synonym for *destined* (often with the negative connotation of
doom), while the second pronunciation is identical to that of
fetid, an adjective meaning dead, rotten, decayed, and stink-
ing. No matter what your political convictions, you are not
likely to wish to imply that Dwight David Eisenhower was
a *fetid* American hero.

fewer / less
-3 VOQ

Fewer applies to number: "There are *fewer* pointy-headed people than flat-headed ones." *Less* applies to situations of volume rather than number—for example, "This soup contains *less* salt than that stew," but "This soup also contains *fewer* carrots." While a native English speaker is not likely to use *fewer* where *less* is called for, many people freely— and erroneously—use *less* where *fewer* is needed.

fiancé / fiancée
-2 VOQ

No, these aren't alternate spellings of the same word. A *fiancé* is a husband-to-be, and a *fiancée* is a wife-to-be. The words are pronounced identically.

fiberglass / fibreglass / Fiberglas
-2 VOQ

In the United States, we spell most -*er* endings with the *e* and *r* in that order, not -*re*, which is the British spelling. In the case of *fiberglass*, you should also be aware that most *fiberglass* is manufactured under a registered trademark, *Fiberglas*, spelled with one *s* and beginning with a capital *F*.

first / firstly
-2 VOQ

First, let us realize that *firstly* isn't wrong, but it should be avoided nevertheless. Why? If you say *firstly*, what happens when you get to the fifty-third item. Does it become *fifty-thirdly*? Use *first*, *second*, and so on.

fiscal / physical   -4 VOQ

You can look pretty dumb if you mix these two up. *Fiscal*
pertains to financial matters. *Physical* relates to the body or
to the material world generally.

flagrant / blatant

See *blatant / flagrant*.

flail / flay   -3 VOQ

Here are two very different words that sound alike and are
therefore often misused interchangeably. To *flail* is to whip,
to flog, or to wave one's arms in a way that suggests a whip-
ping or flogging motion. To *flay* is to tear the flesh away, to
skin.

flair / flare   -3 VOQ

There are two problems here. The first is with the word *flair*
itself. It means a native capacity or an instinctive skill:
"Franklin D. Roosevelt had a *flair* for inspiring mass confidence." It should not be used as a synonym for mere *talent,
ability,* or *aptitude.* It also does not mean stylishness or panache: "He carried out his mission with *flair*" should be
"He carried out his mission with *great style*" or *flash* or
panache.

The second problem is a simple confusion between *flair*
and its homonym *flare,* which, as a verb, may mean to flame
up, to erupt or intensify, to become suddenly angry, or to
expand outwardly ("Bell-bottom trousers *flare* toward the
hems"). As a noun, *flare* may mean a brief burst of light, a
device that produces an intense light used for signaling, an

emotional outburst, an outward expansion, an unwanted reflection in an optical system, a large eruption from the surface of the sun (a *solar flare*), or the area of redness on the skin around the site of an infection.

flammable / inflammable -5 VOQ

Potentially explosive errors may result from misunderstanding the meaning of this pair. If *flammable* means capable of supporting combustion (and it does mean just that), *inflammable* should mean fireproof. Right?

Wrong. Dead wrong.

But *movable* means something like *portable*, while *immovable* means something like *stationary*. A *mutable* thing is subject to change, whereas an *immutable* one is permanent. And so on. Right?

True. If English were 100 percent logical, *inflammable* would, by analogy with many other words, mean incapable of supporting combustion. But it does not. *Inflammable* is a synonym for *flammable*. Avoid confusion by using *flammable* exclusively.

flank -3 VOQ

The meaning of many words grows through simile and metaphor. This is true of *flank*, which, in its primary meaning, denotes the area between the ribs and the hips in animals and, in human beings, the outside of the thigh. Secondarily, by figurative extension, the word may be applied to military situations (a military formation's *flanks* are its sides, as opposed to its front and rear) or to describe situations in which something or somebody is between two things or two people (or two sets of things or people): "The president was *flanked* by Secret Service agents." Since an animal or person has only two *flanks*, the word, in its extended meaning, must also signify something with only two sides. "The president was *flanked* on four sides by Secret Service agents" is nonsense; substitute *surrounded* or *protected*.

flaunt / flout   -3 VOQ

One *flaunts* what one wishes to show off and lord over others. Etymologists do not know where this highly decorative word comes from, but that does not give us the right to *flout* the study of etymology. *Flout* means to show contempt for, and it seems to come from the Old French word for flute—as if playing the flute were a sign of scorn and contempt. *Flaunt* is confused with *flout* very frequently.

flautist / flutist   -1.5 VOQ

While we're on the periphery of the subject of flutes (see the preceding entry), what *do* you call a flute player? *Flautist*—pronounced "flaw-tist"—was once considered the refined word for flute player. That day has passed, however, and *flautist* is now deemed affected. Your best bet: call a flutist a *flutist*.

font / fount   -1.5 VOQ

A *font* may be a baptismal basin, a holy water receptacle (also called a *stoup*), or, figuratively, an abundant source, as in a "*font* of wisdom." To printers and users of word-processing software, a *font* is a complete set of type of one size and face. A *fount* is a fountain, and this word may also be used figuratively in the sense of an abundant source. In

British English, however, *font* and *fount* are used interchangeably.

for   -2 VOQ

Few words are more common than little *for,* and native speakers give it little thought. Yet two questions loom over it.

The first is when to use *for* instead of *because. For* sounds quaint and old-fashioned, maybe even archaic, so many writers and speakers simply avoid it. This is a minor impoverishment of the language, since *for* does serve a different purpose from *because.* Whereas *because* asserts a direct cause-and-effect relationship between the two elements it connects, *for* suggests a less direct relationship. Consider "A frontal attack is a mistake *because* the enemy army is bigger than ours" versus "A frontal attack may be a tactical error, *for* the enemy army is bigger than ours." The first statement embodies certain cause and effect, while the second offers a possible cause and outcome.

If *for* can be a problem because it is *not* used, it can also create unwanted consequences when it *is* used. Consider "Jones was arrested *for* stealing a car" versus "Jones was arrested *for* auto theft." Let's assume the writer embraces the presumption of innocence that is guaranteed to every American citizen. In the context of the first sentence, *for* implies acceptance of Jones's guilt—certainly not the meaning the writer intended to convey. Phrasing it as in the second sentence preserves the presumption of innocence because the *for* states and implies nothing more than the bare fact of Jones's having been arrested for the crime of auto theft. Neither guilt nor innocence is implied—just the fact of the arrest and the reason for the arrest. Be careful how you use *for.*

Although it is a mere three letters in length, it can be a powerfully loaded word.

forbear / forebear -4 VOQ

Big difference between these two. To *forbear* is to shun, but a *forebear* is an ancestor.

forceful / forcible -4 VOQ

These words must not be used interchangeably. *Forceful* is a positive word meaning powerful, effective, energetic, and vivid. *Forcible* is a negative word that means violent and coercive. "The attorney made a *forceful* argument against the *forcible* seizure of his client's assets."

forebearer -4 VOQ

This is a distressingly common error. The correct word is *forebear*, meaning ancestor.

formally / formerly -4 VOQ

Sloppy pronunciation is responsible for a mix-up between these two. *Formally* is an adverb that may be used synonymously with *officially*: "I never introduced you to the president *formally*." *Formerly* is another adverb, signifying something that took place earlier or was the case earlier or in the past: "He was *formerly* president."

former / latter -3 VOQ

Used together, *latter* and *former* are like Roman numerals: official looking, but archaic and confusing. "The accomplishments of Lewis and Clark were extraordinary. The *former* died under mysterious circumstances in 1809. The *latter* lived a long, prosperous life.'' Why not just repeat their names?

As if the confusion weren't enough, *latter* is often misused in place of *last*: "Of Lewis, Clark, and Thomas Jefferson, only the *latter* served in elective office." *Latter* is a comparative and can be used only in the context of two subjects. With three or more, use *last* or *last named*. Better yet, just repeat the name: "only Jefferson served in elective office."

formidable   -2 VOQ

If a fat man wears briefs too small for his waist, sooner or later the elastic will give out. This is the cruel fate in store for *formidable* if users of the language continue to stretch it. The word is meant to convey awe, dread, and fear: "Doing battle with the powerful and skillfully commanded opposing army was a *formidable* prospect." *Formidable* should not be used in more general contexts as a synonym for *large*, *great*, or *significant*: "George has a *formidable* number of friends." With friends like those, who needs enemies?

fort / forte   -3 VOQ

A *fort* is fortified military installation. *Forte*—which is pronounced "fort," and not "fort-tay"—is a person's strong point or particular talent. "While it is true that I am a military engineer, building forts is not my forte." The Italian word *forte*, which *is* pronounced "fort-tay," means loud or strong and is frequently encountered in musical scores as a direction to play loudly.

for the purpose of   -2 VOQ

Use this only if you are getting paid by the word for your writing—in other words, use *for the purpose of* only *for the purpose of* inflating your word count. If, however, you wish to express yourself eloquently and economically, drop the phrase. "I came here *for the purpose of* inquiring about a job" will then become "I came here to inquire about a job."

fortuitous / fortunate   -2.5 VOQ

Fortuitous means happening by chance. Period. It does not imply happening by *fortunate* chance (or unfortunate chance, for that matter). Nevertheless, it is often mistakenly used as a synonym for *fortunate*, doubtless because of its resemblance to that word.

foreword / forward   -5 VOQ

Why so impressive a VOQ? Because *foreword* (meaning an introduction or preface piece at the front of a book, usually written by someone other than the principal author of the book) is often misspelled as *forward* (signifying a location or direction to the front or ahead) and typically misspelled in the worst possible place: at the beginning of a book or other publication. It is there, naked, for all the world to see, to ridicule, and to scorn.

founder / flounder   -4 VOQ

The first problem is with the way *founder* is often misused, in such phrases as "*foundered* and then sank," as if *foundering* were something a ship does before it sinks. In truth, *to founder* is to sink. When a ship *founders*, she's gone. But this usage problem can occur only if *founder* is actually used. Too often, it is confused with the more familiar *flounder*, which, as a verb, denotes a clumsy movement, aimless movement, or a clumsy attempt to move. A watercraft can *flounder,* and such movement may ultimately cause it to *founder,* but the two words have distinct meanings, and one cannot be substituted for the other.

Frankenstein -2 VOQ

In 1818, Mary Wollstonecraft Shelley wrote the novel *Frankenstein, or the Modern Prometheus*, in which one Victor Frankenstein, a Swiss student of occult sciences, cobbles together a quasi-human being out of corpses and body parts he has learned to reanimate. The result, monstrous in appearance, has no name, but has made such an impression on generations of readers and, later, moviegoers, that the scientist's name has come to be transferred to the monster. This is, in effect, a misapprehension and misquotation, which has been perpetuated for almost two centuries now. "United States income tax law is a *Frankenstein* made up of patches bolted to loopholes." Not true! It is a *Frankenstein's monster*.

free gift -3.5 VOQ

A junk mail staple, this phrase is a markedly foolish redundancy, since, by definition, a gift must be free. Also see *true fact*.

frightened of -2 VOQ

Some authorities find this construction acceptable, but, conventionally, *frightened* takes the preposition *at* or *by*, not *of*.

from hence / from whence   -3 VOQ

The concept "from" is contained within *hence* and *whence*, so *from* is superfluous when used with these words. *Hence* means "from here" or "from now," and *whence* means "from which place or position": "We went *hence* to Brookfield, then returned *whence* we had come."

fulsome   -4 VOQ

This word looks good, but what it means is bad. Often misused as a synonym for *copious, abundant,* or *generous, fulsome* actually means insincerely and even offensively flattering. Thus "*fulsome* praise"—the phrase in which this word almost always appears—is not abundant or generous praise but insincere and offensive praise. Also see *noisome*.

further / farther

See *farther / further.*

G

gadfly   -3 VOQ

"She's a social *gadfly.*" It sounds rather charming and is often used in speaking of somebody who knows everybody and attends every party. Unfortunately, this is not what the word means. A *gadfly* is a nuisance, a persistent and irritating critic. In a somewhat more positive sense, a *gadfly* goads others to action—is (to shift metaphors) the proverbial squeaky wheel. Entomologists will tell you that a *gadfly* is an insect member of the family *Tabanidae*; *gadflies* bite and generally annoy cattle and other livestock.

gambit -3 VOQ

Gambit denotes a chess tactic, used at the opening of the game, in which a piece is sacrificed in order to gain a strategic advantage. By extension, the word refers to a concession made to get things under way: "When the labor negotiations were deadlocked, management offered extra vacation days as a *gambit* to restart productive talks." *Gambit* is not a synonym for deception, trick, or trap—though it is often misused as such.

gantlet / gauntlet / gamut -3 VOQ

The constituents of this trio are often tossed up for grabs, to be used and abused in a most confused manner. *Gantlet* is an ordeal or punishment in which the victim or wrongdoer must walk or run between two files of men who beat, club, and kick him. A *gauntlet* is a glove, typically worn by members of the nobility during the age of chivalry. To signify a challenge, a nobleman would fling his *gauntlet* to the ground. *Gamut*, in its primary meaning, is a musical scale. As one may run the musical scale, from *do* to *do*, so someone or something may "run the *gamut*," meaning to experience or display an entire range, whether of emotions, options, opinions, possibilities, choices, or whatever.

gender / sex -? VOQ

There was a time when one could say with certainty that *gender* could not be used as a substitute for *sex*. *Gender* was regarded as strictly a grammatical term, whereas *sex* applied to human beings and came in two varieties, male and female. Since the mid 1970s or thereabout, however, *gender* has been the preferred term for distinguishing *male* from *female,* especially where questions of law are concerned. While *sexual discrimination* is still an accepted phrase to describe situations of bias against men or women because of their *sex*, *gender bias* has gained ground, and people seem generally more comfortable speaking of *gender* rather than *sex*, lest their meaning be mistaken as an allusion to the act of procreation. Miss Nomer suggests that *sex* be used wherever possible to distinguish between male and female; however, she recognizes that it would be quixotic to tilt windmills driven by the prevailing currents of political correctness.

gibe / jibe / jive

See *jibe / gibe / jive.*

glamor / glamour / glamorous / glamourous   -2 VOQ

Dig back to its roots, and you'll find that this word means magic, deceptive charm, a spell of enchantment. No one uses it this way today, and the word has become thoroughly cheesy, an attempt, as inflated as it is vague, to trigger associations ranging from romance to sexiness to prettiness. Thoughtful speakers and writers would do well to avoid the word. Note that, even in the United States, the *glamour* spelling is favored.

For *glamour*, Americans have adopted the *-our* spelling typical of British English, but they've shied away from *glamourous*, perhaps finding two *ou*'s in one word an unacceptable extravagance. Use *glamorous*.

glean   -2.5 VOQ

Carelessly abused as a synonym for *collect* or *acquire*, *glean*
means to gather with great effort from among a scant supply.
This is a figurative extension of the word's primary meaning—to collect the bits of grain left behind by the reaper.

good / well   -4 VOQ

Good is an adjective, which means that its job is to modify
nouns. *Well* is an adverb, which modifies verbs. "You did
good" is illiterate and unacceptable, because *did* is a verb
and *good* an adjective. For the most part, the distinction between adjective-noun and adverb-verb is clear-cut; however,
what about the common phrase "I feel *good*"? Shouldn't
this be "I feel *well*"? *Feel* is a verb, to be sure, and there
is nothing wrong with the second sentence, but most authorities would agree that the first sentence is also acceptable.
The rationale is that the *good* in that sentence modifies *I*, a
pronoun (for grammatical purposes treated as a noun), rather
than the verb *feel*.

gorgeous   -2 VOQ

Women are pleased to be called *gorgeous,* save those readily
offended by the abuse of language. The word should be applied not to human beings but to their adornment. One's
clothing can be *gorgeous*, or one can be *gorgeously* arrayed.
Hair, insofar as it may be regarded as an adornment, may be
called *gorgeous*. For people, use *beautiful, splendid, magnificent,* and the like.

gorilla / guerrilla   -4 VOQ

A *gorilla* is a primate, the largest of the anthropoid apes, whereas a *guerrilla* is a soldier adept at the unconventional and typically stealthy tactics of *guerrilla* warfare. The latter word has its origin in the days of King William's War, fought in North America at the end of the seventeenth century. Louis de Buade, Comte de Frontenac, governor general of New France (Canada), realized that he did not possess the manpower to fight a grand war in the European tradition of one big army pitted against another, so he developed a strategy for what he called *la petite guerre*—a little war. The phrase evolved into the word *guerrilla*, used to denote a limited, covert style of warfare as well as the combatants who fight it. The alternative spelling *guerilla* is acceptable.

got   -2 VOQ

How can you misuse this past-tense form of *get*? By using it in the passive sense, as in "We *got* cheated by the used-car salesman." It is best to avoid this usage, especially in formal writing; however, some authorities actually advocate using *got* in this type of situation if the object of the verb plays a more active role. Here is an example: "Joe *got* in trouble for cheating on his income tax." Joe was not passive, but actively cheated, so *got* may be acceptable here. Also see *have got to*.

gourmand / gourmet   -3 VOQ

Confusion between these two is routine. A *gourmand* is a lover of good food but also a gluttonous consumer of food, good, bad, or indifferent. In contrast, a *gourmet* savors only the best.

graduate   -1 VOQ

Sticklers carp that one does not *graduate* from high school,
but "is *graduated* from high school." Actually, either form
is acceptable. Not acceptable, however, is "He *graduated*
high school."

gray / grey   -2 VOQ

Grey is the British spelling of *gray*, which is the preferred
spelling in the United States. Miss Nomer has encountered
more than one disgruntled U.S. citizen, however, who has
insisted that *grey* "looks" or "feels" more *gray* than *gray*.
Maybe. Nevertheless, *gray* is the preferred spelling on this
side of the Atlantic. Note, however, that the swift breed of
dog that adorns certain long-distance buses is spelled *grey-
hound* on both sides of the ocean.

grill / grille   -1 VOQ

Use *grill* as a verb: "Honey, please *grill* the steaks." Use
grille as a noun: "Dear, I'm putting them on the *grille*." In
a pinch, use them interchangeably.

grisly / grizzly   -2 VOQ

Grizzly means grayish or flecked with gray, but it is most
often used either with *bear* or, alone, as shorthand for *grizzly
bear*. *Grisly* is a synonym for gruesome or ghastly, and while
the sight of a *grizzly* bear outside one's tent may be *grisly*
indeed, the two words are distinct, and the spellings are not
interchangeable. None of this explains, however, why the
grizzly bear is brown and not gray, grayish, or even flecked
with gray.

gun / rifle   -5 VOQ (sometimes)

If you doubt the gravity of the consequences of using *gun*
when *rifle* is appropriate, approach your nearest drill sergeant. The long arm infantry soldiers carry a *rifle*, a weapon
characterized by a rifled (internally threaded) bore. It is most
emphatically *not* a *gun*. That term is properly reserved for a
variety of artillery pieces and may also be used for short
arms, although *handgun* is preferable. Also see *rifle / riffle*.

H

hail / hale   -3 VOQ

To *hail* is to salute or to summon, as when one *hails* a cab.
Hail is also the frozen precipitation that is sometimes associated with severe thunderstorms. *Hale*, as a verb, is derived
from *haul* and is used in such mildly archaic legal phrases
as "*haled* into court," meaning summoned or escorted into
court to answer charges. It is also used in the phrase "to *hale*
from," which indicates one's place of origin or hometown:
"George *hales* from Chicago." As an adjective, *hale* is associated with *whole* and means healthy, as in the phrase
"*hale* and hearty."

handicapped   -2 VOQ

Use "physically challenged" or "person with a disability"
instead of *handicapped*.

harbor / port -3.5 VOQ

"Any *port* in a storm" is really being too choosy, under the circumstances. "Any *harbor* or *port* in a storm" would be more prudent when your ship is threatened with disaster. A *harbor* is any sheltered body of water along the shore that is deep enough for an anchorage, whereas a *port* is a city with a harbor.

hardly -4 VOQ

Hardly is a negative, and since the English language abhors a double negative, it cannot be used with another negative. Often, your ear will tell you when you are making a mistake: "It wasn't *hardly* worth doing" is wrong and *sounds* wrong to most educated users of the language. But a sentence like this can be trickier: "He left without creating *hardly* any impression." *Without* is a negative. The sentence may be revised this way: "He left, having created *hardly* any impression."

hardy / hearty -3 VOQ

These two words are often obscured by careless pronunciation. *Hardy* means strong, healthy, capable of enduring hardship. *Hearty* means from the heart—that is, sincere, unfeigned, unreserved, unrestrained.

harelip -4 VOQ

The proper, and more humane, term is *cleft palate. Harelip* should never be used to describe a person with a cleft palate, as in "He's a *harelip*."

have got to   -3 VOQ

This is a common idiomatic expression that many sensitive speakers find offensive. Why take chances? Delete the *got*. Instead of "I *have got to* go" or "*I've got* to go," say "I have to go" or "I must go."

he   -? VOQ

The generic *he*—the use of the male pronoun to refer to nouns that may designate men as well as women—was unquestioningly accepted at one time. That time has passed, and statements such as "It is the ambition of every physician, no matter who *he* is, to gain more prestige" are no longer acceptable. Physicians may be men or women. Chief executive officers may be men or women. Airline pilots may be men or women. And so on. Yet while users of the language increasingly reject the generic *he*, the language has yet to produce an attractive alternative. The most common alternative is grammatically unacceptable: "Every physician wants more prestige than *they* already have." *They* is neutral with regard to gender, but it is not neutral with regard to number. *Physician* is singular, and *they* is plural. The two cannot be made to work together. Other alternatives are grammatically acceptable, but tiresome or awkward. Repeating *he or she* whenever the generic *he* occurs soon grows tedious, and using *he / she* or *s / he* is clumsy and difficult to read.

Miss Nomer suggests two more pleasing solutions. The first is to find alternative sentence constructions whenever possible—for example, "All physicians want more prestige than *they* already have." This sentence avoids rendering the subject as singular, so the plural—and gender-neutral—*they* is allowed. The second alternative is to alternate *he* and *she* in your writing or speech. Let's say you've written a speech about corporate executives. You have used the generic *he* twenty times. Change ten of those *he*s to *she*s.

heir apparent / heir presumptive   -4 VOQ

The first phrase is often used in general speech. The second rarely. It is a good idea to know what *heir apparent* means before using it, and to understand this term, it is helpful to understand *heir presumptive,* even if you never have occasion to use it. An *heir apparent* is a person whose right to inheritance is assured by law, provided that he or she survives his ancestor. In contrast, the claim of an *heir presumptive* can be defeated if a relative closer to the ancestor is born before the ancestor dies. Thus the king's eldest son is almost always *heir apparent* to the throne. The nephew of a childless king may be designated the *heir presumptive*. He will ascend the throne on the death of the king, if the king fails to sire a son or daughter.

herself / himself

See *myself / herself / himself.*

historic / historical   -3 VOQ

A *historic* event, place, or occasion is memorable, momentous, or in some way outstanding. A *historical* event happened in the past and may or may not be particularly significant. All *historic* events are (or will be) *historical,* but not all *historical* events are *historic*. And before we leave these words, please note that they take the article *a*—a historic occasion—not *an*.

hitherto   -3 VOQ

This is one of those vague, quaint-sounding words that attract
speakers and writers, even if they do not have a firm grasp
on meaning. The word means "until now." This limits it to
situations in the present: "He is spending *hitherto* unheard
of sums" is correct because the situation is a current one,
but "Franklin Roosevelt's New Deal spent *hitherto* unheard
of sums" is incorrect. *Spent* is the past tense of *spend*, and
the events in question took place in the 1930s. Substitute
previously for *hitherto*, and the sentence will be fine.

hoard / horde   -3 VOQ

As a noun, a *hoard* is a secret cache of food or money or
other commodities. As a verb, *to hoard* is to collect such a
secret cache. The connotation is of illegality or, at least, a
lapse of ethics and common decency, as when one *hoards*
food during a famine. *Horde* is always a noun and refers to
a mob, a crowd, a large group, or a swarm. It may also refer
specifically to a nomadic tribe or, even more specifically, to
a Mongol tribe, as in the Golden Horde of Genghis Khan.

holocaust   -3 VOQ

Holocaust should be reserved for situations of destruction by
fire, entailing loss of life. It should not be used as a synonym
for the more general *disaster* or *catastrophe*. Spelled with an
initial capital, *Holocaust* refers to the mass murder of Jews
by the Nazi Third Reich.

home / house   -1 VOQ

A dwindling minority insists on maintaining a distinction between *house* and *home*: *house* is what the architect designs

and the builder builds, while *home* is what those who dwell within the building make of it. If you wish to avoid the wagging finger of some random stickler, you, too, may wish to preserve the distinction between these words.

homogeneous / homogenous -2.5 VOQ

Many assume that the only difference between *homogenous* and *homogeneous* is a variation in spelling and pronunciation, but the words do have subtly different meanings. *Homogenous* (pronounced "home-*mah*-gen-us" or "hah-*mah*-gen-us") things come from the same origin or have the same background: "The isolated population of the island is *homogenous*." *Homogeneous* (pronounced "ho-mo-*gen*-yuss" or "ho-mo-*ge*-nee-us") things share like characteristics: "The upper-class population of the mainland is *homogeneous*."

honesty / integrity -2 VOQ

While they denote closely associated qualities, these words have distinctly different shades of meaning. *Honesty* denotes straightforwardness, moral uprightness, rectitude, fairness, and steadfast resistance to fraud or corruption. *Integrity* denotes adherence to high moral principles and an unwillingness to be swayed by self-interest or other special interests. An *honest* person tells the truth, while a person of *integrity* acts from sound, well-defined ethical and moral principles.

hopeful / optimistic

See *optimistic / hopeful*.

hopefully   **-3.5 VOQ**

This is a perfectly fine adverb, provided that you mean to
say "in a hopeful manner": "I asked her for a loan and then
gazed into her eyes *hopefully*." Vast hordes use *hopefully*,
however, as a sentence adverb in the sense of "it is to be
hoped" or "I hope": "*Hopefully,* she will lend me the
money." Careful writers and speakers find this use of *hope-*
fully quite offensive, but they cannot say why. In truth, this
use is justified by analogy to other adverbs: "Mercifully, she
loaned me the money," and "Frankly, I'm relieved that she
loaned me the money." Nevertheless, the most judicious
users of the language will tell you that "Hopefully, she will
lend me the money" is a bad sentence. Miss Nomer's advice? Stop beating your head against the wall, bow to irra-
tional pressure, and drop this use of *hopefully* from your
vocabulary. Put it this way instead: "*I hope* that she will
lend me the money."

How come?   **-3.5 VOQ**

How come? is a question that will raise no one's eyebrows
when spoken, but that may well be reviled bitterly if written.
In writing, use *Why?* and spurn *How come?*

human   **-2 VOQ**

Human is an adjective, *human being* a noun. "I am only
human" is correct, but "I am a *human*" misuses an adjective
as a noun. "I am a *human being*" is correct.

hung / hanged   **-1.5 VOQ**

One of the more bizarre byways of the English language is
the past and future tenses of *hang* when the verb refers to

the death penalty—that is, to execute by hanging: "The judge *hung* a picture of his mother on the wall of his chambers, then entered the courtroom, where he pronounced sentence on the accused, ordering that he be *hanged* by the neck until dead."

hutspah / hutzpa / chutzpah / chutzpa

See *chutzpa / chutzpah / hutspah / hutzpa.*

I

I / me   -4 VOQ

Whenever Miss Nomer hears a sentence beginning "Between you and *I*," she tunes out whatever follows. She admits to a nasty prejudice against people who cannot distinguish between subject and object. *I* is nominative, which means that it is reserved for use as the subject of a sentence. When you need an object, choose *me*: "*I* hit him after he hit *me*." *I* is the actor; *me*, the acted upon. When used with the preposition *between*, the first person pronoun must be in the objective case: "Between you and *me*." Please see the entry on *between / among.*

-ics words   -3 VOQ

English includes a host of words ending in *-ics*—*physics, logistics, tactics, mathematics, politics,* and so on. Are these to be treated as singular or as plural? The answer is an equivocal sometimes singular, sometimes plural. Theoretically, the applicable rule is simple. If the word denotes or is used as a subject (in the sense of a field of study) or a science, it is treated as singular: "*Physics* was Marie Curie's passion." If the word denotes or is used in the sense of practical activities or qualities, it is treated as plural: "The *logistics* of moving our headquarters were complex." In practice, however, this distinction is not always easy to make. Some words are always used in the sense of a subject or science, but many may be used this way as well as to denote a practical activity, and this can lead to indecision—for example, "*Logistics* was always General Sherman's concern," or "*Logistics* were always General Sherman's concern." Either sentence may be correct, depending on context and the meaning intended. The first sentence means that General Sherman was always concerned with the study of the subject of *logistics*, whereas the second sentence means that he was always occupied with practical questions of how he was going to supply his army as it marched from one place to another.

ideal / idyllic   -2 VOQ

Ideal has several meanings, including the conception of perfection; the standard or model of perfection; a goal, a worthy principle or aim; highly satisfactory, just right, perfect. *Ideal* may also mean lacking practicality, imaginary, existing only in the mind. *Idyllic* is the adjective form of *idyll,* which may be a brief literary work evoking a pastoral or pleasantly rural scene; the scene itself; or a carefree or romantic interlude or episode. "Bob was raised on a beautiful and tranquil farm. He had an *idyllic* childhood. Perhaps that's why he is an *ideal* father to his two sons."

ideology -3 VOQ

To begin, a note on pronunciation. The *i* in *ideology* is pronounced like the *i* in *idiot,* not the one in *ideal.* Beyond this,
note that the word's primary meaning is specialized, a term
used by philosophers to describe the science of ideas. In
more general use, *ideology* denotes a body of belief, doctrine,
and myth belonging to a large social group, institution, social
class, or social movement. Democracy, capitalism, and communism are *ideologies.* The word is not a synonym for *idea*
or even for a set of *ideas* or *beliefs* or *doctrines,* unless these
are held in common by a large historically or socially significant group. "The *ideology* behind the design of the new
personal computer is revolutionary." In this sentence, *ideology* should be replaced by *thinking, concept,* or some similar word.

idiot / imbecile / moron -4 VOQ

What is sufficiently offensive about these terms to merit a
-4 VOQ? They are never to be used as synonyms for a person
who is developmentally disabled. Beyond this caution, be
aware that the three words do have distinct meanings. Strictly
speaking, an *idiot* is a person with a mental age equivalent
to under three years; an *imbecile* has a mental age equivalent
to a child between three and seven years old; and a *moron*
possesses a mental age equivalent to that of a seven- to
twelve-year-old.

i.e. / e.g. -4 VOQ

These are abbreviations of the Latin phrases *id est* (that is)
and *exempli gratia* (for example); therefore, they have quite
distinct functions. Compare "Mussolini was wounded in the

gluteus maximus—i.e., the buttocks" with "A number of dictators have met with embarrassing accidents—e.g., Mussolini." Note that it is not necessary to italicize these abbreviations. And now that you understand how and when to use them, consider not using them at all. Instead of *i.e.*, use "that is," and for *e.g.*, use "for example." The plain English equivalents of the Latin abbreviations are easier to understand and more elegant.

if / whether   -3 VOQ

This pair is often used indiscriminately; however, in standard English, *if* expresses a simple condition, whereas *whether* is used to express doubt or to ask an indirect question that expresses conditions. A few examples will make these distinctions clear. "We will leave tomorrow morning *if* it does not rain" expresses a simple condition. "I don't know *whether* I'll go tomorrow" expresses doubt. "I want to know *whether* you intend to go with me tomorrow" is an indirect question. Note that none of the *whether* examples includes the phrase *or not* ("I want to know *whether or not* you intend to go"). The *or not* is redundant and should be avoided, except when you need to put equal emphasis on the alternatives: "You will go *whether* you like it *or not*."

if and when   -3 VOQ

"We'll cross that bridge *if and when* we come to it." Drop either the *if* or the *when*, and the meaning of this cliché will emerge unharmed. Prune deadwood lest your prose wither and die.

ilk -2 VOQ

Ilk means similar kind or class or stripe. It is often used in conjunction with *that*: "others of *that ilk*." It must never be used with *like* or *similar*—"with others of *similar ilk*"—because to do so would be redundant. There is also a mistaken belief that the word is vaguely disparaging, probably because politicians have carelessly thrown it about in campaigns of disparagement: "We don't want Brady and his *ilk* in City Hall!" In itself, the word has neither negative nor positive connotations, but it has been used so often in negative contexts that many readers and hearers impute a negative slant to it. For that matter, *ilk* has been used often, period. It rings rather hollow and may be regarded as a cliché. You can't go wrong simply avoiding the word altogether.

illegitimate child (daughter, son).

See *bastard / illegitimate child (daughter, son) / natural child (daughter, son).*

illusion / allusion

See *allusion / illusion.*

illusion / delusion -2 VOQ

If an *illusion* is a mistaken or erroneous perception or belief, a *delusion* is a downright false belief or opinion. A *delusion* is more sinister than an *illusion* and connotes lack of emotional balance and even mental derangement: "Laboring under the *delusion* that he was Napoleon, he began issuing orders to an army that was, of course, an *illusion*.'' Never speak of a ''false delusion''; by definition, a *delusion* is false.

immanent / imminent / eminent

See *eminent / immanent / imminent*.

immigrant / emigrant / émigré

See *emigrant / immigrant / émigré*.

immigrate / emigrate

See *emigrate / immigrate*.

immoral / amoral   -4 VOQ

Loose talkers swap these as if they were variations on the same theme. They are not. To be *immoral* is deliberately to flout ethics and decency, to do the opposite of what is good. To be *amoral* is to lack a sense of ethics. It is to be without morality. A person who knows the difference between right and wrong, carefully plots a crime, and then executes that crime is *immoral*. The person who suffers from a mental incapacity that deprives him of the knowledge of right and wrong may commit a similar crime, yet must be described as *amoral*. Another way to express the difference between the two words is to equate *immoral* attitudes and actions with a contrariness to established standards of morality, and to equate *amoral* attitudes and actions with an indifference to such standards.

immure / inure / inter -3 VOQ

Perhaps none of these words are in the everyday vocabulary of most people, and perhaps for that very reason they are often confused. *Immure* means to wall up, as the protagonist in Edgar Allan Poe's famous short story "The Cask of Amontillado" does to avenge himself on a man who, in some obscure way, has wronged him. More figuratively, the word may be used as a highfalutin synonym for *imprison*. *Immure* should not be used as a synonym for *burial*. That is the province of *inter* (pronounced "in-TUR"). While *immure* and *inter* are at least related in meaning, *inure* has an entirely different meaning from either word; however, it does sound like *immure* and for that reason is frequently confused with it. *Inure* means to become so accustomed or habituated to some situation, behavior, or action that it no longer has an effect: "Her off-pitch singing used to drive me crazy. I had fantasies of *immuring* her or otherwise doing her in and *interring* her remains in the backyard, but now I find that I am *inured* to the sound of her voice."

impact -4 VOQ

This word has serious problems, or, rather, many people create serious problems by misusing it. *Impact* should be reserved to denote forceful collision, whether of physical bodies or opposing ideas or points of view. It may also be used in situations in which an action has a very powerful effect: "The tax legislation will have an *impact* on all homeowners in the state."

Now, for the problems. *Impact* can be used as a verb, but it should be used as such only in instances of physical collision: "When will the meteor *impact* the earth?" Hordes of government officials and journalists have pressed the word into ugly service in contexts like this: "The tax legislation will *impact* all homeowners in the state." Use *affect* instead. Indeed, even when *impact* is used as a noun, it should be employed sparingly, only in situations that warrant such a powerful word instead of *influence* or *affect*.

Impacted may be used as a verb to denote physical collision: "A meteor that *impacted* the earth millions of years ago may have contributed to the extinction of the dinosaurs." As an adjective, however, *impacted* means packed or forced close together. An *impacted* wisdom tooth, for example, is wedged in the alveolus (tooth socket) so tightly that it cannot erupt normally. It causes pain, and is therefore usually removed by a dentist or oral surgeon. It is incorrect to apply *impacted* as an adjective meant to designate the equivalent of an affected area: "The electrical outage has been repaired, and power has been restored to all *impacted areas*." Wrong! Use "*affected* areas."

impeach   -4 VOQ

"No United States president has ever been *impeached*." Not true. While no president has been removed from office, one, Andrew Johnson, was *impeached*. To *impeach* is to charge a public official, formally and before an authorized tribunal, with wrongdoing. A possible outcome of such a charge may be removal from office, but to be *impeached* is merely to be charged, not ejected. In other contexts, to *impeach* may mean to accuse or to challenge or attempt to discredit. The latter meaning is common in the courtroom: "The defense attorney was able to *impeach* the testimony of the prosecution's lead witness."

implement -1.5 VOQ

Go ahead, use this verb if you must; just be aware that it is generally orotund. "We will *implement* new procedures" can be said more powerfully as "We will *introduce* new procedures." Wherever possible, find a more direct, less abstract, less pompous replacement for this word.

implicit / explicit

See *explicit / implicit.*

important / importantly -2 VOQ

A sentence modifier is a word, phrase, or clause that modifies an entire sentence rather than a particular word or clause. *Important* functions as a sentence modifier in something like this: "Most *important*, never shift into reverse while moving forward." As a sentence modifier, use *important* rather than *importantly.*

impose

See *assess.*

impossible / impassable / impassible -3 VOQ

An *impossible* thing cannot exist, and an *impossible* task cannot be accomplished. A road buried in an avalanche is said to be *impassable,* which does mean, however, that it is *impossible* to traverse. A person who is unfeeling or passive is said to be *impassible.*

imposter / impostor   -2 VOQ

Although American spelling tends to favor *-er* over *-or* endings, we spell *impostor* with an *-or*.

impracticable / impractical   -2 VOQ

Impracticable, which many find almost impossible to pronounce, means infeasible. While theoretically possible, perhaps, an *impracticable* operation cannot actually be carried out. *Impractical* enterprises may be technically feasible, but they are not worth doing or are not sufficiently valuable in practice: "You could erase what's written on that paper and reuse it, but that would be *impractical.* Start with a fresh sheet." A thing can be both *impracticable* and *impractical.*

in behalf

See *behalf.*

in / into   -2.5 VOQ

In is not simply a shorter version of *into.* Ponder the difference between "Claire walked *in* the room" and "Claire walked *into* the room." In the first sentence, whether the writer intended it or not, Claire is already inside the room, walking. In the second sentence, she clearly walked into the room from the outside. Generally speaking, verbs of motion require *into,* unless you wish to denote interior motion, as in the first Claire sentence.

include   -2.5 VOQ

Take care how you use this word. It implies incompleteness, as in "The original Mercury astronauts *included* Alan Shepard, Gus Grissom, and Scott Carpenter." There were seven Mercury astronauts in all, so this sentence uses the past tense of *include* correctly. If the four other astronauts were added to the list, it would be far better to substitute *were* for *included*.

incredible / incredulous   -2.5 VOQ

Think in terms of synonyms. For *incredible*, the synonym is *unbelievable*. For *incredulous,* it is *skeptical.*

inculcate / inoculate   -4 VOQ

To *inculcate* is to teach, to impress a concept or doctrine upon one or more people. To *inoculate* is to administer a biologically active material into an organism, usually to provide protection against an infectious disease. In an unforgiving world, it is a bad mistake to confuse the two.

indefinitely   -3 VOQ

Many use this word as a vague substitute for the concept of long duration, as when the salesperson coos: "How long will this widget last? *Indefinitely.*" But *indefinitely* means without known or specified limits, so *indefinitely* may be a very long time—or a very short time or some span of time in between.

Indian / Native American   -1.5 VOQ

Ever since Christopher Columbus refused to admit that he had not landed in Asia—the so-called East Indies—the world has been confused about the word *Indian*. That's what Columbus called the people he encountered in October of 1492: Indians, natives of the East *Indies*. While few Indians object to being called such, scholars and historians certainly prefer *Native American* to *Indian*. It is also appropriate to use the term *Native people(s)* or *Native American people(s)*, which takes in Eskimos (Inuits) and Aleuts as well as *Indians.* Also see *native / Native.*

indict / arraign   -3.5 VOQ

These words apply to different parts of the same process. To *indict* is to charge with a crime, and to *arraign* is to summon before a court to answer the *indictment.*

indiscreet / indiscrete   -3.5 VOQ

Most of the time, when you use this word, you mean *indiscreet*: imprudent, not to be trusted with secrets or sensitive or embarrassing information. *Indiscrete* is a perfectly good word, too, but it is rarely used. It is applied to something that is of a piece rather than separated or separable into distinct (*discrete*) parts or sections. Also see *discreet / discrete.*

individual   -4 VOQ

The use of *individual* and *individuals* in place of *person* and *people* has never greatly disturbed Miss Nomer; however, it sets on edge the yellowed teeth of many a grammarian and usage maven, and for this reason it merits a serious -4 VOQ. To avoid giving ammo to the carpers, use *person* or *people* instead of *individual* or *individuals*. The only exception arises when you need to distinguish persons from a group or class—for example, ''The new tax law will benefit corporations as well as *individuals*.''

induce / deduce / adduce

See *deduce.*

inequity / iniquity -4 VOQ

There is major potential for embarrassment in the misuse of these similar-sounding words. *Inequity* is unfairness or injustice, whereas *iniquity* is immorality. Prostitutes may ply their trade in a den of *iniquity*, not a den of *inequity*.

infectious / contagious

See *contagious / infectious*.

infer / inferred / inferring / inference -4 VOQ

Let's look at what these words are *not*. They are not an alternative way of saying *imply, implied, implying, and implication*. But many misguided souls use them as if they were. If, in great indignation, you turn to your political opponent and ask, ''Are you *inferring* that I am a liar?'' you are really asking if he is concluding from evidence or premises that you are a liar. Nothing all that wrong with this, except it's not remotely what you wanted to say. To *imply* is to hint at or to express something indirectly, and this is hardly the same thing as to draw conclusions from facts or assumptions.

To *infer* is to apply a logical process (of drawing conclusions from evidence or premises), whereas to *imply* is simply to hint at something or to express something indirectly.

inflammable / flammable

See *flammable / inflammable*.

ingenious / ingenuous   **-4 VOQ**

Careless readers stumble over these with great frequency.
Ingenious means clever or brilliant, as in an *"ingenious* device." *Ingenuous* means sincere, without guile. The opposite
of *ingenuous* is *disingenuous*.

innocent / not guilty   **-2 VOQ**

No American jury has ever found a defendant *innocent*. In a
legal context, the opposite of guilty is *not guilty*, which
means nothing more or less than that, in the jury's opinion,
insufficient evidence was presented to deem the accused person guilty of having committed the crime charged. In contrast, *innocent* implies much broader concepts, including
absolute blamelessness and a complete absence of corruption,
sin, malice, or wrongdoing. The word may also mean innoc-
uous, neither dangerous nor harmful. It may mean inexperienced or naive, lacking guile. It may even mean ignorant, as
in "My accountant seems to be *innocent* of any knowledge
of the U.S. Tax Code." The versatile *innocent* may mean
unaware ("He was *innocent* of all the trouble his actions
caused her") or lacking ("We were served a soup totally
innocent of flavor). *Innocent* may even be used as a noun to
denote someone free from evil, sin, or guile, or to denote an
entirely inexperienced, unworldly person: "She was a sweet
innocent."

innovation / invention   **-2 VOQ**

Innovation is the introduction of something new; however,
the connotation of *innovation* is not as sweeping and revolutionary as that of *invention*. Whereas *invention* denotes the
creation of a previously nonexistent device or process, *in-*

novation suggests an improvement on existing technology. Deciding when to use one word or the other is not always a matter of black and white, but often involves judgment. Most would agree, for example, that the automobile was an important *invention*, whereas the automatic transmission was a significant *innovation* in automotive technology.

A further note: The word *new* should never precede *innovation* or *invention*. Since both *innovation* and *invention* embody the quality of newness, the addition of *new* would be a pleonasm—utterly and unforgivably redundant.

in order to -3 VOQ

This one's a bad habit that's difficult to shed. In almost all cases, *in order to* can be reduced simply to *to*: "Press the button *in order to* operate the machine" is wordier but no clearer than "Press the button *to* operate the machine."

inquire / enquire

See *enquire / inquire*.

in regards to -4.5 VOQ

What a nasty expression! It is both illiterate and ugly. Use *regarding* instead: "*Regarding* our conversation, Mr. Smith, I will pursue the solutions you suggest."

insane -1.5 VOQ

To casual speakers and writers, *insane* is a synonym for *crazy, mad, loony, bonkers*. That's fine. Just be aware that, although the word has no place in the modern practice of psychology or psychiatry, it does have a very specific meaning to those in the legal profession. To a lawyer or other jurist, an *insane* person is afflicted with an unsoundness of mind sufficient to render him or her unfit to maintain a contractual or other legal relationship. Usually, a person judged *insane* cannot be considered legally responsible for acts committed. An *insane* person may be remanded to the custody and care of a mental health facility, even against his or her will.

insidious / invidious   -3.5 VOQ

Something *insidious* is corrupting or deceitful in an especially stealthy manner. An *invidious* thing or action is hateful and offensive as well as unfair, as in an "*invidious* comparison"—the phrase in which the word most frequently occurs.

insight about   -3 VOQ

Insight can stand alone, but when it needs a preposition, use *into*, not *about*: "Mary can provide us with *insight into* the workings of the organization."

insure / assure / ensure

See *assure / ensure / insure*.

in terms of   -4 VOQ

Contemporary prose is plagued by this phrase. It is a circumlocution, an expression that "walks around" the meaning rather than jumps into it directly. It is almost always possible and desirable to substitute *about* or *concerning* or some other equally simple single word: "Let's talk *in terms of* (about) salary." "He was speaking *in terms of* (about) cost efficiency." "What do you think we should do *in terms of* (concerning) price?" A sentence like "Where do we stand *in terms of* the deadline?" should be thoroughly overhauled and streamlined: "Will we meet the deadline?"

in the midst of   -2 VOQ

This phrase is not only rather clumsy, it is also vaguely archaic or at least old-fashioned. *Amid, in, inside,* or *within* usually will serve more effectively: "*In the midst* (amid) of the noise and confusion, I misplaced my wallet." However, the phrase may still be useful for indicating immersion in a process or action: "We are *in the midst of* revising the contracts."

invent / discover

See *discover / invent.*

invoke / evoke

See *evoke / invoke.*

irony / sarcasm   -3.5 VOQ

Careless writers—no! careless *thinkers*—utter these interchangeably. *Irony* uses words to express something different from, and usually the direct opposite of, what is really meant. If for example, your spouse backs the car into a fire hydrant, you may turn to him or her, and exclaim, "Nice driving!" That's irony. It also happens to be *sarcastic,* but *sarcasm* does not always rely on *irony.* It can consist of ridicule, cutting remarks, and caustic humor as well as *irony.* A neophyte scriptwriter asked a Hollywood veteran how long he should make the summary of his proposed script. "Keep it under ten pages," the old hand advised. "Any more than that, and the producer's lips get tired." That's *sarcasm*—and not a trace of *irony* in it.

irregardless   -5 VOQ

This is one of those words that sound as if they should exist and that, on the face of it, have every right to exist. The trouble is, this word does not exist, nor has it ever existed. A mutant, it was most likely spawned on the analogy of *respective* and *irrespective* or maybe even *flammable* and *inflammable*. If these word pairs can exist, why not *regardless* and *irregardless*? That, after all, seems only fair. But, then, language is not a court of law and is under no obligation to dispense justice. Therefore, when tempted to say *irregardless*, just say *regardless* or, if you must, *irrespective of*.

Because *irregardless* is a multisyllabic non-word, uttering it brings the very worst disgrace and disaster.

irritate / aggravate

See *aggravate / irritate*.

its / it's   -4 VOQ

These minuscule words are frequent victims of careless abuse. *Its* is the possessive of *it,* whereas *it's* is a contraction of *it is.* "*It's* against the law to rob a bank of *its* money." The reason for the frequent confusion is obvious: English possessives characteristically take an apostrophe—but, then, so do contractions. Here is a case where the apostrophe indicates a contraction and therefore cannot be used also to indicate possession.

J

jailer / jailor   -2 VOQ

Jailor somehow looks "more right" than *jailer*, but in the
United States, spellers tend to favor *-er* endings over *-or*
endings, so *jailer* it is.

jealousy / envy

See *envy* / *jealousy*.

jerry-built / jury-rigged   -3 VOQ

These terms express related but distinct ideas. A *jerry-built*
device or structure is one that has been cobbled together
hastily and cheaply. The materials are characteristically
flimsy and the workmanship shoddy. (*Jerry* is British slang
for *defective*.) A *jury-rigged* item is a temporary device or
structure quickly put together in an emergency, using whatever materials and workers are available. To *jury-rig* is to
make an emergency repair, to improvise. A makeshift quality
is implied, but not shoddiness. *Jury-rigged* comes from the
days of sailing ships, when a *jury sail* or a *jury rig* was a
temporary or makeshift repair made at sea.

Jew / Jewish   -1 VOQ

A Jew calls himself a *Jew*, not a *Jewish* person, which may
even be perceived as a mildly offensive attempt at euphe-

mism. Note that *Jewess* is unacceptable. Use *Jew* for both
men and women.

jibe / gibe / jive   -3 VOQ

Jibe and *gibe* are variant spellings of the same word; however, spelled *gibe*, the word usually means to make taunting,
derisive remarks. As a noun, a *gibe* is a taunting or derisive
remark. While the word in this sense may also be spelled
jibe, that spelling is usually used to mean "in accord with"
or "in agreement with," as in "Joe's account of the matter
jibes with yours." A specialized meaning of *jibe* is nautical,
meaning to shift a fore-and-aft sail from one side of a vessel
to the other while sailing before the wind in order to sail on
the opposite tack. The word may be used as a noun to describe the nautical act of *jibing*. If, as a landlubber, you are
confused by this definition, you may be tempted to dismiss
it as so much *jive*, a term once used by jazz musicians, especially African-Americans, to describe nonsensical, glib, or
deceptive talk. As an adjective, *jive* suggests a phony or
worthless quality: "Don't make me read that *jive* book." The
same musicians who coined the word as a term of derision
also applied it to a style of swing music of the 1940s and
early 1950s, and *jive* was sometimes used to describe the
very jargon jazz musicians used among themselves. *Jive*,
then, is word rich with meaning, but none of those meanings
is equivalent to *jibe*.

join together   -2 VOQ

Do not *join* these two words. *Together* they are redundant.

judgement / judgment
-2 VOQ

Some people have trouble accepting the amputation of the vowel after the *g* in this word. The British won't hear of it. But here in America we prefer to pass *judgment* rather than *judgement*.

judicial / judicious
-3.5 VOQ

Judicial relates to judging in general or to the legal system in particular: "There is much to admire and much to deplore in our *judicial* system." *Judicious* means prudent, exhibiting sound judgment: "A *judicious* decision is the product of careful analysis and dispassionate thought."

jurist / juror
-4 VOQ

Both of these words are derived from the same Latin root, *ius*, meaning *law*; however, the similarity ends there. A *jurist* is a professional thoroughly educated in the law. The term most aptly applies to an eminent judge whose knowledge of the law is both practical and theoretical. In contrast, a *juror* is, by definition, a legal layperson, who is serving on a jury.

K

karat / carat / caret / carrot

See *carat / caret / carrot / karat*.

kibbutz / kibitz   -3.5 VOQ

A *kibbutz* (pronounced kĭBOOTS) is the type of collective
farm found throughout Israel; the word is derived from the
Hebrew *qibbus* (gathering). The plural is *kibbutzim. Kibitz* is
not Hebrew, but a Yiddish word freely imported into English
and meaning (negatively) to look on idly at an activity—
often a card game—and offer unwanted and annoying advice, or (more positively) to engage in idle chitchat.

kilt / kilts   -2 VOQ (-5 VOQ among Scots)

Both a *kilt* and a pair of pants are masculine attire, but the
similarity ends here, including in number. A *kilt* worn by one
person is singular, whereas *pants* are always plural. Reserve
kilts to designate two or more garments.

kin   -3 VOQ

Kin is a collective plural, denoting relatives. It should not be
used to designate an *individual*. ''I am his *kin*'' should be
''I am one of his *kin*.''

klatch / klatsch

See *coffee klatch*.

Kleenex / kleenex

See *Xerox / xerox*.

knot / knots   -4 VOQ

For sailors and sometimes for aviators, the *knot* is a unit of speed. Unlike the mile, it is not a unit of distance; therefore, "twenty-five *knots* per hour" is wrong, and "twenty-five *knots*" is correct.

kudo / kudos   -2 VOQ

The word is rather tired now and should be put to bed, but if you must use it, you have to include the *s*. There is no such thing as a *kudo*.

L

lambast / lambaste   -3 VOQ

Some authorities accept *lambast*—pronounced to rhyme with *clam cast*—as a legitimate alternative to *lambaste*—pronounced to rhyme with *clam taste*. Most agree, however, that *lambaste* is not only preferred but correct.

latter / former

See *former / latter*.

lawyer / attorney / counsel / counselor

See *attorney / lawyer / counsel / counselor*.

lay / laid / lie   -5 VOQ

A vast proportion of the English-speaking world slept
through this particular grammar lesson. Splash cold water on
your face, take a swig of black coffee, and read on. In addition to its other meanings, *lay* is the past tense of *lie* (in
the sense of recline): "He *lay* down and fell asleep." *Lay*
also serves as the present tense of a transitive verb meaning
to put or place: "Please *lay* your weapon down!" A transitive verb always takes an object—in this case, *weapon*. *Lay*
must have an object; thus "I am going to *lay* down," which
lacks an object, is incorrect and should be "I am going to
lie down." However, you could say, correctly, "I am going
to *lay myself* down," because *myself* is the object of *lay*. *Lay*
is most often misused in the imperative mood, like this: "*Lay*
down!" The correct imperative is "*Lie* down!" However,
you could say "*Lay* yourself down!"

   That leaves us with *laid*. It is the past tense of *lay* (when
lay is regarded as a present-tense verb meaning to place or
put): "They *laid* their weapons down."

lead / led   -4 VOQ

Lead may be pronounced "led" and, pronounced this way,
refers to the soft, malleable metal with an atomic weight of
207.19 and an atomic number of 82. It may also refer to the
graphite writing material in a "lead" pencil. Pronounced
"leed," *lead* is the present tense of *led*. Thus pronounced,
lead means to show the way by going in advance. The word
also has related meanings, all turning on the sense of being
foremost or most important, and all pronounced "leed."

leave / let -4 VOQ

Leave is fine as a substitute for *let* in such phrases as "*let* (or *leave*) him alone"; however, *leave* cannot be substituted for *let* in the sense of allow or permit: "*let* (not *leave*) me go," "*let* (not *leave*) me be," "*let* (not *leave*) us not fight over it," or "*Let* (not *leave*) sleeping dogs lie."

legitimize / legitimise / legitimate -2 VOQ

Begin by rejecting *legitimise*, a British spelling, in favor of *legitimize*, the U.S. spelling, but then consider the verb *legitimate*. (Unlike the adjective, pronounced so that the last syllable sounds like *mitt*, the last syllable of the verb is pronounced "mate.") Many usage authorities, as well as conscientious writers, always on the lookout for alternatives to *-ize* words, suggest that *legitimate* replace *legitimize*. This seems like a good idea to Miss Nomer, though she will not press the point, except in one specialized application. Historically, the procedure whereby the father of a child born out of wedlock marries the mother and adopts the child is called *legitimation,* not *legitimization*, and the verb form is *legitimate*, not *legitimize*: "The king sought to *legitimate* the child by adopting him."

leitmotif / leitmotiv -2 VOQ

The word was popularized by the nineteenth-century German composer Richard Wagner to denote a melodic passage associated with a specific character, idea, or situation. The meaning of the word has been extended to include any dominant or recurring theme in a work of art or even in history: "Containment of communism was a *leitmotiv* of the Cold War years." While both spellings are accepted by most au-

thorities, it is preferable to use the German original, *leitmotiv*,
in which the *v* is pronounced (as in German) like an *f*. In
other words, spell the word *leitmotiv*, but pronounce it *leit-
motif* ("light-moteef").

lengthy   -3 VOQ

Lengthy is a limp substitute for *long*. Why bother with it?

less / fewer

See *fewer / less*.

lest   -4 VOQ

Be careful with this creaky old word. It is brittle and might
just break. *Lest* is not the simple equivalent of "so that." It
means either "for fear that" or "so that such-and-such will
not or would not": "Pat transferred his wallet to his jacket
pocket *lest* he fall victim to a pickpocket." The sentence may
be seen as the equivalent of "Pat transferred his wallet to
his jacket pocket *for fear that* he would fall victim to a pickpocket" or of "Pat transferred his wallet to his jacket pocket
so that he would not fall victim to a pickpocket." The meaning of the sentence would be badly distorted if *lest* were seen
as the equivalent of "so that" (without the "not"), yet *lest*
is often misused in precisely this way: "Pat transferred his
wallet to his jacket pocket *lest* he *not* fall victim to a pickpocket."

levee / levy   -2.5 VOQ

Unless you are a tax accountant or an IRS agent, you probably don't use *levy* every day, and, if you don't live on a

flood plain, it is unlikely that *levee* is a part of your daily speech. So it is little wonder that these two words are frequently misused. To *levy* is to impose or to collect a tax; as a noun, a *levy* is an imposition or collection of a tax—a "tax *levy*." The word may also mean to confiscate property as part of a legal action, but, used this way, the verb is intransitive and does not take an object. Secondarily, *levy* may mean to draft into military service or to wage war, and, as a noun, *levy* may refer collectively to the troops who are drafted. A *levee* is an embankment intended to prevent a river from flooding. It may also be a landing area for rivercraft. An embankment mounded around an irrigated field is also called a *levee*; its function is to keep water in, rather than out.

Should you have found yourself in the presence of royalty some two hundred or more years ago, you might have been summoned to a royal reception held immediately upon the king or queen's rising from bed. This *levee* comes directly from the French *lever,* a rising, but it is sometimes a misnomer, since the royal personage may receive visitors while remaining supine—that is, in bed, without rising. Today, British royalty still holds *levees*, but these are simply informal afternoon audiences granted in an upright, not supine, position.

liable / libel / slander -4 VOQ

If you publish a *libel*, you are *liable* to be sued. *Libel* is false publication—in writing, in print, or on billboards (in signs or pictures)—that maliciously damages a person's reputation. For something to be *libelous*, it must be false, it must be malicious, and it must be shown to be injurious to the victim's reputation. *Slander* is similar to libel, except that the communication is oral rather than written or printed. Both *libel* and *slander* may be used as nouns or verbs.

Liable is an adjective meaning legally obligated or at risk of suffering adverse consequences or an unfavorable outcome. "This court will hold you *liable* for your actions," or "Don't play with fire. You are *liable* to get burned." Also see *apt / liable / likely*.

lightening   -4 VOQ

An obnoxious misspelling of *lightning*. This is very widespread, quite embarrassing to the miscreant who makes the error, and thoroughly offensive to the tender sensibilities of those who stumble across this abomination. Do note, however, that *lightening* is a word: "Alphonse aimed at *lightening* his load and therefore discarded his first-edition copy of *Valley of the Dolls* but took care to retain his trusty *Miss Nomer's Guide to Painfully Incorrect English*."

like / as   variable VOQ

The *traditional* grammatical rules governing the use of these words are straightforward and immutable. *Like* is a preposition, which is used in comparing nouns and pronouns: "She (a pronoun) looks *like* a horse (a noun)." "She (a pronoun) is like me (a pronoun)." And so on. *As* is a conjunction, which is used to introduce clauses: "It looks *as* if he might succeed." (The clause introduced is "if he might succeed.") "Do *as* I say, not *as* I do." (The clauses are "I say" and "I do.") Miss Nomer insists that you cannot go far wrong if you adhere to tradition, but, in some cases, even Miss Nomer admits that tradition has come to seem too stiff and stuffy. Those of a certain age may recall the advertising slogan of a cigarette brand: It "tastes good, like a cigarette should." Well before public health officials sounded the alarm over the links among smoking, cancer, and heart disease, grammarians wailed about the pervasive slogan's use of *like* where *as* was called for. Normal people (as opposed to grammarians) countered that nobody really talks this way: "tastes good, *as* a cigarette should." And the truth is, would you rather spend social time with a person who said "I've eaten so much, I feel *like* I weigh a ton" or one who put it this way: "I have consumed so large a quantity of nourishment that I feel *as* if I weigh 2,000 pounds"? Let common sense help you here—common sense and context. In formal situations, exercise care to ensure that you use *as* when you need a subordinating conjunction. Informally, however, let your ear direct you, and say what *sounds* right.

likely   -3.5 VOQ

Likely looks like an adverb (it ends in -*ly*), but it can also function as an adjective: "Sarah is a *likely* candidate for promotion." Used as an adverb, *likely* requires the aid of *very*, *quite*, or *most*: "She will *most likely* be promoted." *Likely* cannot stand alone as an adverb. "She *likely* will be promoted" is incorrect.

likewise   -3.5 VOQ

An adverb, *likewise* is so often misused as a conjunction that, shameful though it is, such misuse may raise surprisingly few eyebrows. Here's the problem. "I repaired the widget, the framiss, the locking valve, *likewise* the locking pin." The proper word here would be *and* or perhaps the phrase *as well as*. As an adverb, *likewise* should refer to the manner in which something occurred or an action was done: "I repaired the widget, the framiss, and the locking valve with a left-handed monkey wrench, then repaired the locking pin *like-wise*.''

limited   -2 VOQ

This vague term has been pressed into service by Madison
Avenue to mean brief or soon to expire: ''Available for a
limited time only. Act now!'' Actually, the word means nothing more or less than within limits or within bounds. Its
opposite is *infinite*.

limpid   -3 VOQ

This word has nothing to do with the quality of being limp—
or weak or frail—but means crystal clear: ''Her eyes were
limpid pools.''

linchpin / lynchpin   -2 VOQ

This word, used to denote the central, key, cohesive element
in an organization, a speech, an argument, or a program,
verges on being a cliché; take warning. When you spell it,
use the preferred *linchpin*, although most authorities do accept *lynchpin* as a variant. The figurative use of the word is
based on the *linchpin* inserted at the end of a shaft or axle
to keep a wheel or gear from slipping off.

lion's share   -2 VOQ

This expression is a cliché, which is reason enough to avoid
using it, but if you feel you must indulge, at least refrain
from employing *lion's share* as a synonym for *most* or *majority*. The phrase comes from a fable of Aesop, in which
the *lion's share* is not a share at all; it is everything or very

nearly everything. The phrase, therefore, has an element of irony. Reserve it for extreme cases: "Controlling 99 percent of the market, Acme Widget clearly held the *lion's share* of the business." At 60 percent, the phrase would be inappropriate. At 80 percent? A judgment call.

liquefy / liquify   -2 VOQ

Trigger-happy pedagogues pounce on *liquify* as a misspelling of *liquefy*, even though most dictionaries accept it as a legitimate variant. Miss Nomer understands that *liquefy* just "doesn't look right," but it is the preferred spelling. Use it.

litany   -3.5 VOQ

Habitually misused as an alternative to *list, long narrative*, or *history*, *litany* should be applied only to instances of tedious, repetitive recitation. In its original sense, the word denotes a type of prayer in which priest and congregation engage in alternate responses. "The prosecuting attorney read the *litany* of the defendant's crimes" is acceptable if the intention is to suggest that the crimes were so numerous and of such similar nature that recitation of them was tedious. If, however, the crimes enumerated were varied and spectacular, the use of *litany* would be incorrect, even if the list were long. Similarly, to speak of the "*litany* of action and adventure in T. E. Lawrence's *Seven Pillars of Wisdom*" is at best an oxymoron. True, Lawrence of Arabia's autobiography is very long, but it is hardly a mere recitation. If the user of *litany* wishes to say that he was bored by one adventure after another, the word may be accepted as an intentional oxymoron; otherwise, it is used incorrectly.

literally   -2 VOQ

Literally has been overused to death or, as many would put
it, has been overused *literally* to death. In fact, it is not only
overused, but overused incorrectly (as here) in the sense of
figuratively, which is precisely the opposite of what *literally*
means. No word can be worked to death *literally*, because
words are not living organisms to begin with. Certainly, however, a word like *literally* can be *figuratively* worked to death.

livid   -3 VOQ

Livid is so often used as an intense alternative to *enraged*
that some people think it is a synonym for *angry* or that it
describes the flaming red flush that one often sees in a raging
person. The latter association is particularly dangerous because it leads to such expressions as ''*livid* flames,'' with
the intended meaning of orange-red. The trouble is that *livid*
means the color of lead and, by extension, severely black-
and-blue or purplish, the color of bruised flesh: ''He bore a
livid wound.'' If you give the writer credit for knowing what
he's saying, you must see the wound as a severe bruise. But
might he have meant to describe a bright red gash marked
by inflammation? Beware.

loan / lend   -1 VOQ

Exercise a degree of caution in using *loan* as a verb. Meticulous writers and speakers regard it exclusively as a noun:
''I need a *loan.* Would you *lend* me money, please?'' Most
of the English-speaking world is comfortable with *loan* as a
noun or a verb: ''Yes, I will *loan* you some money.'' But it
is nevertheless prudent to observe the *loan / lend* distinction
in formal writing and formal speaking contexts.

loath / loathe   -2.5 VOQ

Loath is an adjective synonymous with *reluctant* or *disinclined*, as in "I am *loath* to go to the dentist." *Loathe* is a verb, synonymous with *despise*: "I *loathe* going to the dentist." The final *e* makes all the difference. These are *not* merely alternative spellings. But here's a lucky break. The two words are pronounced identically: "lowth" (with the *th* voiced, as in *that*). This means you won't be found out unless you put it—wrong—in writing.

longshoreman / stevedore   -2 VOQ

Unless your business involves shipping, you probably don't use either of these words much and you think about them even less often. Just don't approach a *stevedore* and call him a *longshoreman*. A *longshoreman* is a laborer who loads and unloads ships. A *stevedore* is his employer.

loosen / unloosen   -2 VOQ

Use either of these, and you'll be understood to mean *untie* or *make less tight*; however, many people regard *unloosen* as overly colloquial or just plain silly. After all, if *loosen* is to untie, shouldn't *unloosen* mean to tie or tighten? Use *loosen*, and avoid *unloosen*. (But take a look at *ravel / unravel*.)

lousy   -3 VOQ

Be aware that *lousy* means infested with lice. Of course, it is widely used to mean dirty, nasty, disgusting, poor, badly made, inferior, not feeling well, and the like. But it should be reserved for informal occasions, when slang is appropriate. Many people find it a harsh and unpleasant word.

love child   -3 VOQ

To denote a child born out of wedlock, *love child* was once a popular alternative to *bastard* or *illegitimate child*. Most speakers and writers find it excessively coy, however, and it should be avoided. *Natural child* is the best alternative to *love child, illegitimate child,* and *bastard*. See *bastard / illegitimate child (daughter, son) / natural child (daughter, son)*.

lumber / timber

See *timber / lumber*.

luxuriant / luxurious   -2 VOQ

Luxuriant is synonymous with *abundant growth*: "The jungle was *luxuriant* with thick foliage." *Luxurious* pertains to luxury: "The rock star's vacation home, in the midst of a *luxuriant* jungle, was *luxurious*."

M

madam / madame -3 VOQ

In English, *madam* is used as a courtesy title in addressing certain officials—Madam Ambassador, for example, or Madam Chairman (yes, Chair*man*). It is also a courteous form of addressing a stranger—the feminine equivalent of *sir*: "Please step this way, *madam*." A *madam* is also the keeper of a brothel. *Madame* is a French word and is properly used as a courtesy title or a form of address for a woman in a French-speaking area only.

major -3.5 VOQ

Major means greater in importance or significance or size than other things, events, or issues of the same class. It should not be used in place of such words as *important*, *significant*, *serious*, and the like. Thus "He was a *major* influence on me," while not incorrect, is poor usage. Either "He was the *major* influence on me" or "He was an *important* influence on me" is better, depending on whether the speaker means that the subject of the sentence was her most significant influence or one of several significant influences. *Major* should never be preceded by a qualifier, such as *more, less,* or *very*.

majority / plurality   **-3.5 VOQ**

The *majority* rules? Not always. Sometimes a *plurality* is
sufficient. The *majority* is most of the total. A *plurality* is
most of any subset of the total. The concept of a *plurality*
is important, for example, when more than two candidates
run for an office and none receives a *majority* of the total
votes: "In the election of 1860, Abraham Lincoln received
1,866,452 votes. His three major opponents received a total
of 2,815,617. Lincoln won a *plurality* of votes, not the majority." Note that *majority* is often preceded by the article
the and that *plurality* is usually preceded by *a*, which reflects
its status as a relative quantity rather than an absolute.

mandatory / compulsory

See *compulsory / mandatory*.

mankind   **-3 VOQ**

Substitute *humankind* for this sexist term.

manmade   **-3 VOQ**

Substitute *artificial, manufactured,* or *synthetic* for this sexist
term.

martyr for   **-2.5 VOQ**

As a noun, *martyr* takes the preposition *to*, not *for*: "Nathan
Hale is regarded as a *martyr* to the cause of American in-
dependence." As a verb, *martyr* does take *for*: "Joan of Arc
was *martyred* for the freedom of France."

masterful / masterly -2 VOQ

The distinction between these two words continues to blur; however, careful writers, readers, and listeners still respect it. *Masterful* means domineering, whereas *masterly* means skillful or expert: "Churchill was a *masterful* leader but a *masterly* politician."

matinee performance -2 VOQ

A *matinee* is a daytime performance; therefore, tacking on the word *performance* is redundant. Drop it.

may / might -3 VOQ

Much *may* (or *might*) be said about these two words, but in everyday use the distinction between them comes down to this: *may* allows possibility, whereas *might* allows less possibility or, conversely, more uncertainty: "If you don't pay your parking fines, the city *may* take you to court, and you *might* lose your license." The city has the power to take scofflaws to court and routinely does so; a possible—albeit remotely possible—outcome of such action is loss of a driver's license. Also see *can / may*.

may be / maybe -3 VOQ

May be is a verb phrase. It means *possibly is* or *perhaps will be*: "It *may be* too late to register." Combined into a single word, *maybe* is an adverb that means *possibly*: "*Maybe* it's too late to register."

mean / median / average

See *average / mean / median*.

means   -2 VOQ

This word offers some challenge to a user deciding whether
to treat it as a plural or singular. As a synonym for financial
resources, *means* is always regarded as plural: "His *means*
are adequate." But when *means* is used in the sense of an
agency by which one attains an end, the word may be treated
as plural or singular. You need to rely on your ear: "All
possible *means* are at your disposal," but "Every *means* of
rescue was tried."

meantime / meanwhile   -3.5 VOQ

It is simple to keep the use of these words distinct if you
remember that *meantime* is a noun and *meanwhile* is an adverb. *Meantime* is the intervening period: "In the *meantime*,
I occupied myself by reading *Miss Nomer's Guide*." *Meanwhile* pertains to the intervening period or signifies at the
same time: "*Meanwhile,* I occupied myself by reading *Miss
Nomer's Guide*," or "The surgeons are operating; meanwhile, we must pray."

    Meanwhile is a most useful word, when it is properly used.
Meanwhile always expresses a chronological or time-related
relationship. It may not be used to express any other relationship or as a mere transition from one subject to another:
"Mary Shelley wrote *Frankenstein* in 1818. *Meanwhile*,
Boris Karloff starred in Hollywood's version of the story in
1931." Ugh! "Frankenstein is the name of the scientist who
created the monster, but *meanwhile*, most people call the
monster by that name." Ugh! Ugh!

media / medium -3 VOQ

Media is the plural of *medium*. It is correct to speak of the "television and print *media*," but not of the "television *media*." It is, after all, but one *medium*.

mediator / arbitrator

See *arbitrator / mediator*.

menial -2 VOQ

Menial is not a neutral adjective to describe laborers or their work. It is clearly disparaging. Especially to be avoided is using the word as a noun: "Don't talk to him. He's just a *menial*."

mental -1.5 VOQ

Mental pertains to the mind and all that is associated with the mind. Too often it is used when *emotional* would be far more accurate: "How do you feel *mentally*?" would be better expressed as "How do you feel *emotionally*?" *Mental* is also an insensitive slang term for emotionally disturbed or mentally ill: "He's *mental*" or "He's a *mental* case."

mentally retarded -4 VOQ

Most find this term offensive. Use "developmentally disabled" instead.

meretricious / meritorious   -4 VOQ

It is a never-failing source of amazement and amusement that the English language affords many similar-sounding words with opposite or nearly opposite meanings. *Meretricious* sounds a great deal like *meritorious*, which means worthy of merit; however, if *meritorious* is rooted in *merit*, *meretricious* traces its ancestry to the Latin *meretricius*—''of prostitutes.'' The English word is a metaphorical extension of this original Latin meaning: plausible but insincere, specious (as in ''a *meretricious* argument''), or attracting attention with a vulgar, showy display. It is a bad mistake to confuse the *meretricious* with the *meritorious*.

meticulous   -1 VOQ

Meticulous is so commonly misused that most of us are hard-pressed to identify the misuse as such. Most of us understand the word to mean extremely careful. Generally, we use the word to praise an admirable quality: ''Felix Mendelssohn was a *meticulous* craftsman.'' Yet the root meaning of the word, founded on *metus* (Latin for *fear*) is overly careful, fearful, hesitant, and timorous, as if fearing error. If you are *meticulous* in how you use the language, you may wish to avoid the word as a term of praise.

microwavable / microwaveable   -2 VOQ

Nature, it is said, abhors a vacuum, and most English writers abhor compound words in which the final *e* of the first part of the compound ends up next to another vowel. Hence *microwaveable* is usually spelled *microwavable*.

might of
-5 VOQ

Like *could of,* this is an illiteracy and unacceptable in all circumstances. The correct phrase is *might have.*

millennia / millennium
-3 VOQ

Latin plurals give English speakers trouble from time to time. *Millennia* is a plural and indicates two or more thousand-year periods. The singular is *millennium.* Isn't *one* thousand years enough for you?

minimal
-2 VOQ

Careless speakers and writers throw this word around as a stand-in for *very little.* That's not what it means. *Minimal* conveys the idea of the *least possible.*

minimize
-2 VOQ

"You always *minimize* my accomplishments!" Thus one complains to one's spouse, in the belief that *minimize* means to belittle or make light of or dismiss as inconsequential. But it means none of these things. To *minimize* is to reduce to the minimum, to reduce to the least possible number or degree. In the sense the disaffected spouse intends, use *belittle* instead, reserving *minimize* for something like the following: "Applying a thin coat of the paint *minimizes* drying time." Also note that since *minimize* means to reduce to the minimum, it is incorrect to tack on to the word such qualifiers as "as much as possible."

minion / minyan   -2.5 VOQ

A *minion* is a follower, an underling, a servant, or a minor
public official. These meanings may seem strange inasmuch
as the word is derived from the French *mignon*, ''darling.''
However, the word can also mean one who is highly es-
teemed or highly favored—an idol. Far more specialized,
minyan is the minimum of ten men whose presence orthodox
Jews deem a quorum for public worship.

mobile / movable / portable   -2.5 VOQ

All three words relate to motion, but in significantly different
ways. *Mobile* describes a vehicle or other object that is designed for motion, whereas *movable* describes an object that
is not designed for motion, but that can be moved. A temporary housing unit, for example, is *movable*, but neither
mobile (unless it is a trailer on wheels or a recreational vehicle) nor *portable*. *Portable* things are specifically designed
to be *movable*; *portability* implies that the object can be
moved by one person.

mold / mould / molding / moulding   -2.5 VOQ

Mold is American English, and *mould* is British English.
That should be a simple enough distinction; however, some
writers labor under the misapprehension that there is something special about the decorative architectural element called
molding and insist that it be spelled *moulding*. Not so in the
United States. *Mold* is *mold*, and *molding* is *molding*.

molt / moult   -2 VOQ

One hears little conversation about *molting*, unless one is
among bird or snake fanciers. For that reason, the word al-

ways looks unfamiliar, and it is easy to be bullied into using the British spelling, *moult*. Be firm. In the United States, we spell it *molt*.

money / moneys / monies   -1.5 VOQ

Money, like *herd*, is normally a collective noun; however, when you refer to more than one kind of national currency or to funds from various sources, *moneys* may be used: "The charity received *moneys* from three sources." Although most words ending in -*y* take -*ies* as a plural, *moneys* is the preferred plural.

monolithic / monumental   -2.5 VOQ

Monolithic and *monumental* are related in meaning, but nevertheless distinct from each other in connotation. Both may be used to describe large, impressive architectural structures as well as, more figuratively, massive undertakings, ideas, and projects. In architecture, a *monolith* is literally a single stone, and a *monolithic* structure is a massive, tall building without ornamentation of any kind. Figuratively, a *monolithic* concept is characterized by great scope but narrow— and therefore erroneous or misguided—thought or intent. A *monumental* building may be noble and majestic in addition to massive. A *monumental* project or idea may also be noble and majestic as well as large in scope; however, the word may also describe some large undertaking that is not necessarily useful. In some instances, *monumental* may be entirely negative: "The eighty-million-dollar motion picture was a *monumental* flop."

moot   -1.5 VOQ

Everybody knows that a *moot question* is one that's academic
or useless or hypothetical: "The decision has been made and
is final, so any questions about the matter are now *moot*."
Well, no. Actually, *moot* is another of that handful of words
almost everyone uses to mean one thing when it actually
means another. *Moot* means subject to discussion or open to
debate, which is almost the opposite of what *hypothetical* or
academic implies—that the question may be argued but that
there is no practical point in doing so. Miss Nomer's advice
is to use this word sparingly and with care. You'll be understood if you use *moot point* or *moot question*, but most
likely you'll be understood because, like almost everyone
else, you are misusing the word.

moron / idiot / imbecile

See *idiot / imbecile / moron*.

most   -1.5 VOQ

Avoid using *most* as short form of *almost*: "*Most* all of us
are delighted." Sticklers find it irritating.

muchly   -4.5 VOQ

Have you ever received a memo or letter signed "Thanks
muchly"? Miss Nomer has, and she doesn't like it. *Much*
serves as both an adjective and an adverb, so the *-ly* ending
is unnecessary, illiterate, and suffocatingly cute. Don't ever
use it.

Murphy's Law / Peter Principle / Parkinson's Law
-4 VOQ

Miss Nomer is tired of hearing these misused. *Murphy's Law* is named for the American engineer Edward A. Murphy, who, in 1958, formulated the following observation: Anything that *can* go wrong *will* go wrong. Named by and for Canadian-born educator Laurence J. Peter in 1968, the *Peter Principle* is Peter's observation that, in any hierarchical organization, employees rise (are promoted) to the level of their incompetence.

Now that we have that straight, on to Parkinson's Law. Formulated in 1955 by C. Northcote Parkinson, an English historian, this is an observation that, in any office setting, the number of subordinates tends to increase at a fixed rate, regardless of the amount of work produced. The second part of the law is better known: Work expands so as to fill the time available for its completion.

mutual / common

See *common / mutual*.

myself / herself / himself
-2 VOQ

Consider this: "Three of us went—Joe, Mary, and *myself*." In such contexts, use the simple personal pronoun *I* rather than the clumsy *myself*. The same holds true for *herself* and *himself*: use *she* and *he*.

N

nation / country

See *country / nation*.

native / Native   -2 VOQ

Spelled with a lowercase *n*, the adjective *native* means inborn, innate, natural to, or belonging to a particular place by birth; as a noun, *native* signifies a person born in a particular place or indigenous to a place: ''Abe Lincoln was a *native* of Kentucky.''

Until recently, Caucasian Europeans and Americans referred to indigenous Africans as *natives*, and the word became equated with supposedly primitive or backward people. In this sense, *native* is condescending and offensive. It should not be used. However, *Native*, with an uppercase *N*, is widely accepted as a substitute for *American Indian*. Used this way, *Native* is usually combined with *American* or with *people*. See *Indian / Native American*.

Native American / Indian

See *Indian / Native American*.

natural child (daughter, son).

See *bastard / illegitimate child (daughter, son) / natural child (daughter, son)*.

nauseated / nauseous   -3 VOQ

"I'm *nauseated* because clam chowder is *nauseous* to me."
If you feel as if you are going to vomit, you are *nauseated*.
The cause of your affliction is *nauseous,* or *nauseous* to you.
If this distinction is difficult to remember, think of *poisoned*
versus *poisonous*. The first refers to the condition, the second
to the substance that caused the condition.

Neandertal / Neanderthal / Neandrathal   -3 VOQ

While the *th* in this word may be pronounced as *th* or as *t,*
the vastly preferred spelling is *Neanderthal*. A few authorities accept *Neandertal*, but only a few. No one who knows
paleontology accepts *Neandrathal*, because it is just plain
wrong—the result of a common mishearing of the word.

Although *Neanderthal* is widely used to describe any
crude or boorish person (with the manners of a cave dweller),
it should be used with care when applied to actual prehistoric
human beings. *Neanderthal* is not a generic term for a cave
dweller or a prehistoric person. It applies specifically to a
member of the extinct species *Homo neanderthalensis*, a
name that comes from the Neanderthal Valley of Germany,
where skeletal evidence of this being was first found.

near future   -1.5 VOQ

Be aware that, while this phrase may be useful when it is
necessary to distinguish between a *near* future and a *distant*
future, it is most often a wasteful expression. Whenever possible, use *soon* or *shortly* instead of "in the *near future*."

née   -3 VOQ

This French word means "born." It has been imported into
English, but never fully made part of the language. Using it,
therefore, is sometimes awkward. To begin with, one is born
with one's family name only; the first name is bestowed
some time after birth. It is therefore incorrect to write "Ellen
Jefferson, *née* Ellen Smith." The woman's name is properly
"Ellen Jefferson, *née* Smith." A second problem with this
French import is that it is a feminine adjective, which means
that sophisticated readers and listeners will be scandalized,
or at least amused, by its application to a man: "John Jefferson, *née* Smith." Remember, *née* means "born"; it does
not mean "formerly known as," which is the very phrase
you should use in reference to a man who has changed his
name.

neither . . . nor   -4 VOQ

You assume a certain responsibility when you use the *neither
. . . nor* construction, and that is an agreement to obey the
law of correlative conjunctions. Compliance with this law is
not as intimidating as it sounds, as this example demon-
strates: "My decision depends *neither* on you *nor* them" is
incorrect because the proposition *on* is missing. Correct the
deficiency this way: "My decision depends *neither* on you
nor on them." Or this way: "My decision depends *on neither* you *nor* them."

nevertheless / never the less / nonetheless /
none the less   -3.5 VOQ

These are always written as one word: *nevertheless, none-
theless.*

niggard / niggardly   -5 VOQ

There is nothing wrong with these words. A *niggard* is a miser, a mean and stingy person; as a verb, *to niggard* is to treat someone in a miserly way. The adverb *niggardly* means miserly. There is a problem, however, if any of these word forms is confused with the supremely offensive racist pejorative, *nigger*. Linguistically, *niggard, niggardly*, and *nigger* are unrelated. *Niggard and niggardly* come from Old Norse via Old and Middle English, whereas *nigger* is derived from the French and the Spanish words for the color black. Nevertheless, the words sound so much alike that potentially hurtful confusion of meaning could result. Be careful.

noisome   -3 VOQ

Noisome does not mean noisy or annoying, but disgusting and offensive: ''The crowded and filthy slums of eighteenth-century London were notorious as *noisome* places that bred disease, crime, and despair.'' Take a look at *fulsome*, too.

nominal   -2.5 VOQ

''For a *nominal* fee'' does not mean ''for a small fee,'' but for a fee so small as to be insignificant—that is, a fee ''in name only,'' which is what *nominal* means. A *nominal* fee or *nominal* charge, therefore, should be almost nonexistent. If it is, in fact, substantial, the word has been misused, and the pitchman (or pitchperson) is taking you for a ride.

none   -2 VOQ

Hard-liners stubbornly insist that *none* is, in effect, a contraction of *not one* and therefore must take a singular verb:

"Of the many choices, *none is* attractive" instead of "*none are* attractive." In truth, *none* is not the contracted equivalent of *not one*, but is a synonym for *no amount* or *not any*. Often, a plural verb is desirable, and sometimes one is even required: "*None* of the preparations *were* completed." *Preparations* is not readily reducible to a singular *preparation*, and, in any case, it is unlikely that the writer intended the meaning that all but a single item of preparation was completed. A similar example: "The commander has complained that *none* of his *forces are* ready for action." Again, *forces* is not readily rendered as a singular in this context, so treating *none* as such is not only awkward but incorrect.

Having pointed out the fallacy of rigidly regarding *none* as singular, Miss Nomer must now warn you that coupling it with a plural verb may nevertheless provoke carping. Her advice? Unless there is a clear grammatical reason to pair *none* with a plural verb, bow to the pressure and use a singular.

noone / no one   −5 VOQ

An astonishing number of people otherwise apparently sound of mind are afflicted with the delusion that *no one* is one word or that it may at will be rendered as one word: *noone*. This is one of the stupidest-looking injuries that can be inflicted on the language. *Noone* dumbfounds readers, who are likely to see it as a *faux*–Middle English version of twelve P.M. ("ye highe noone").

nosey / nosy   −2 VOQ

Why not just tack on a *y* to *nose* to get *nosey*? You could, and some authorities would accept it. Most, however, insist on *nosy*.

nostalgia   -2 VOQ

In its root sense, *nostalgia* means homesickness, but its meaning has been universally extended to denote the pleasurable, albeit sometimes bittersweet, yearning for the bygone. Be careful not to stretch this already fully extended word any further, however. It is not a synonym for *longing* or *yearning*. Nor should the word be slapped onto *things*: "The old movies—now that's *nostalgia* for you." *Nostalgia* denotes a feeling, an emotion, not the cause of the feeling.

notable / noted / notorious   -2 VOQ

Notable and *noted* may be used interchangeably, except that *notable* may be used especially for newcomers on the scene who are worthy of notice, whereas *noted* should be reserved for people who are already well known. *Notable* and *noted* are positive in connotation, while *notorious* is negative, signifying a person or other entity well known for reprehensible reasons: "the *notorious* outlaw Jesse James."

noxious / obnoxious   -3.5 VOQ

No, these aren't variations on the same word. *Noxious* is normally applied not to human beings but to corrosive, harmful, injurious, or highly unpleasant substances, as in the phrase "*noxious* fumes." *Obnoxious* is often applied to human beings who are highly offensive, hateful, or in some other way objectionable. The word may also be applied to animals ("an *obnoxious* little dog") and to inanimate objects ("an *obnoxious* little dress"). Note that fumes, for example, may be *obnoxious* (offensive and disgusting) or *noxious* (harmful).

number / amount

See *amount / number*.

O, Oh   -1 VOQ

O or *Oh* may be used as vocatives—forms of address—and *oh* may be used as an exclamation. As a vocative, both *O* and *Oh* are capitalized, and *O* is not followed by punctuation: "*O* Lord, hear my prayer!" Only *oh* should be used as an exclamation, and in this sense, it is not capitalized unless it begins a sentence. It is followed by punctuation—either a comma or an exclamation point: "*Oh,* please. I don't want to hear any of that nonsense," or "*Oh!* spare us your lame excuses!"

oblivious   -1 VOQ

Oblivious means forgetful, unconcerned, unmindful of, or no longer mindful, unaware, or not conscious of. Most of the time, we hear or read the word paired with *to*: "He was *oblivious* to criticism." The fact is, straitlaced language watchers insist that the word means only forgetful or no longer mindful, and they further insist that it be paired exclusively with *of*: "He was *oblivious* of her beauty." Miss

Nomer believes that the broader sense of *oblivious*, now so widely used and understood, is quite acceptable, and that the word may be used with *to* or *of*. She draws the line, however, at using the word without a preposition and object, as in "The stupid girl was *oblivious*."

obnoxious / noxious

See *noxious / obnoxious*.

obscene / pornographic   -3.5 VOQ

"Surely these are peas in a pod!" you exclaim. Well, no, not at all. *Obscene* pertains to anything or any action that is offensive, abhorrent, and generally contrary to accepted standards of morality and behavior. *Pornographic* is narrower in its meaning, because it pertains specifically to material (publicly printed, broadcast, spoken, exhibited) that is without artistic merit, scientific interest, or educational value, but is intended exclusively to titillate and to arouse sexual desire.

observance / observation   -3 VOQ

Observance signifies either taking note of something or acting in accordance with duty or custom, as in "In *observance* of Memorial Day, the bank will be closed on Monday." *Observation* is the equivalent of a viewing or a perceiving of something: "A clear night is best for *observation* of the stars."

obsolescent / obsolete   -2.5 VOQ

The difference between these two is a matter of degree. An *obsolescent* process, idea, or device is on its way toward becoming out of date, or *obsolete*. An *obsolete* process, idea, or device is already outdated, technology, the state of knowledge, or the state of the art having passed it by. Note that *obsolescent* can be expressed as a comparative—"This aircraft is more *obsolescent* than that one"—but *obsolete* is an absolute.

obviate / obvious   -4 VOQ

Despite superficial similarity, this pair is unrelated. *Obviate* is a verb meaning *prevent* or *avert*. *Obvious* is an adjective that means immediately apparent. "We took steps to *obviate* obvious hazards."

odalisque / basilisk

See *basilisk / odalisque*.

official / officious   -4 VOQ

While one may encounter any number of *officious officials*, the two words have distinct meanings, and to confuse them is quite embarrassing. *Officious* is an adjective used to describe someone who is meddlesome and overly eager to offer unwanted help and advice. As an adjective, *official* means authorized or authoritative; as a noun, it signifies a person who is duly authorized to perform certain functions, render certain services, or make authoritative judgments and decisions about certain matters. Interestingly, *officious* once had a positive connotation, describing someone who was eager to serve. Alas, this meaning has evaporated, and the word is wholly pejorative nowadays.

ogle -1.5 VOQ

This lovely word is often the victim of mispronunciation. Though she has rarely been *ogled* herself, Miss Nomer has repeatedly heard the word inexplicably mangled as "oogle." Pronunciations rhyming with "focal" or with "boggle" are correct.

okay / ok / OK / O.K. -2 VOQ

None of these is desirable in formal writing, but if you do use *okay*, write it out rather than content yourself with the abbreviations.

old adage / adage

See *adage / old adage*.

on account of -2 VOQ or -5 VOQ

Used as a substitute for *because of*, the phrase *on account of* is only mildly offensive (-2 VOQ): "The game was canceled *on account of* rain." Certainly the phrase should be shunned in formal writing; however, it must be banished utterly as a substitute for *because*: "She wrote to me *on account of* she was so awful lonesome." This is illiterate (-5 VOQ).

on behalf

See *behalf*.

one and the same -2 VOQ

This familiar phrase is both wasteful and trite—in short, a bore. The first two words can almost always be eliminated without doing harm to meaning. "Mark Twain and Samuel Clemens were *the same* person."

only   -4 VOQ

Be careful where you put *only* in a sentence. It should be positioned immediately before the word you want it to modify. In *The Careful Writer*, Theodore M. Bernstein quotes a well-known example of the power of placement. Consider: "I hit him in the eye yesterday." Now try putting *only* in the eight places available in the sentence. Each of the possible placements produces a different meaning, depending on which word *only* modifies.

ophthalmologist / optometrist / optician   -2 VOQ

These three terms for eye-care professionals are not synonymous. An *ophthalmologist* is a medical doctor, an M.D., who specializes in treating disorders of the eye. An *optometrist* holds a doctor of optometry (O.D.) degree and is properly addressed as "Doctor," although he or she is not a medical doctor. The *optometrist* is trained and licensed to examine the eyes for defects and to prescribe corrective lenses; however, he or she may not prescribe medicines or treat the eye in any other way. An *optician* makes and/or sells eyeglasses and contact lenses. Rarely encountered today is *oculist*, an archaic term for a practitioner who treats disorders of the eye.

opinion / estimation

See *estimation / opinion*.

opposite / contrary

See *contrary / opposite*.

oppress / repress / suppress -3 VOQ

The common thread that ties these terms together is the idea of involuntary restraint. To *oppress* is to inflict hardship on someone or, more usually, on a group. The word has strong social and political connotations and can be applied only to human beings: "Totalitarian governments *oppress* the people." If *oppress* is social in scope, *repress* is highly personal. It usually refers to an attempt to deny recognition or expression of one's feelings and desires: "It is unhealthy to go through life *repressing* your true feelings." Finally, *suppress* is the most general of the words conveying restraint. It may be applied to people, animals, actions, feelings, or things: "In 1775, the British took steps to *suppress* the growing rebellion in North America."

optimistic / hopeful -2 VOQ

Optimists are by their nature *hopeful*, but *optimistic* and *hopeful* have different meanings. Use *optimistic* to describe a general attitude, an approach to life that views everything in the sunniest possible light. Use *hopeful* to describe specific situations. "Joe is always smiling and never seems to be unhappy. His outlook is perpetually *optimistic*." Contrast "Joe lost his wallet with all of his money in it, but he was *hopeful* that it would be found and returned to him, money and all."

oral / verbal -2 VOQ

Verbal means "in the form of words" and, as such, can be used to describe spoken as well as written communication, although it is almost always used to describe spoken communication. *Oral* unmistakably refers to spoken communication. If you wish to make yourself unambiguously clear, use *oral* rather than *verbal* when you mean to describe spoken communication. Also see *aural / oral*.

ordinance / ordnance / ordonnance   -3 VOQ

An *ordinance* is a law, usually at the local or municipal level; it may also be a decree, authoritative rule, or, in a military context, a command or order. *Ordnance* is a military term meaning weapons and other equipment, especially large guns. Less frequently encountered, *ordonnance* refers to the structure or arrangement of the elements of a literary, artistic, or architectural work.

Orient / Oriental   -3 VOQ

These are old-fashioned terms for Asia and Asian and should now be avoided because many Asians regard them as the condescending product of an era when much of Asia was under European colonial domination. Use *Asia* and *Asian* instead. Note that *Oriental* as a noun is more strongly offensive—very nearly a racial slur. In the absence of knowledge of a person's specific country of origin (China, Korea, Japan, etc.), *Asian* is perfectly acceptable as a noun to denote a native of an Asian country or one whose ethnic heritage is Asian.

orient / orientate   -2.5 VOQ

Both of these words are acceptable in the sense of to align or position something or oneself to get one's bearing; however, *orientate* often provokes irritation among fastidious writers and speakers. They insist that it is incorrect. While this is not true, *orientate* does sound clumsy, striking the ear as a word carelessly cobbled together. Use *orient* instead.

other / else

See *else / other*.

otherwise   -3.5 VOQ

Otherwise is often plucked as a vague word to serve the needs of lazy people: "You must decide on the plan's merits or *otherwise*." Why not just say "flaws"? Take the time and effort to find the right word instead of an empty substitute.

overexaggerate   -4 VOQ

Both an illiteracy and linguistic overkill, *overexaggerate* is to be shunned and eschewed utterly.

oversight   -4 VOQ

A terrible thing has happened to this word. The government's gotten hold of it and turned it into something it was never intended to be. Thus an official body charged with the responsibility of overseeing something is dubbed—with quite unintentional comedy—the *Oversight* Committee. Although some dictionary writers have loyally sided with our government, Miss Nomer contends that *oversight* should not be used as the noun counterpart of *oversee*. An *oversight* is a mistake, an error, an unintentional omission, not a descriptive term for the function of *overseeing*.

P

palate / palette / pallet   -3 VOQ

Here is a trio of troublesome homonyms. *Palate* is the roof of the mouth; it also refers to the sense of taste, as in "pleasing to the *palate*." *Palette* is the board on which an artist blends paints. The word may also refer to the range of colors in a painting or to the colors that are characteristic of a particular artist. *Pallet* is sometimes seen as an alternate spelling of *palette*, but it primarily refers to a portable platform on which cargo is placed, making it easier to handle, especially by forklift. A *pallet* is also a hard, narrow *bed*; southerners use the word to denote a temporary bed consisting of bedding arranged on the floor. "Make me a *pallet* on the floor," an old southern blues lyric goes.

panacea   -3 VOQ

A *panacea* is a cure for all ills; therefore, the word cannot be correctly applied to a cure for a single malady or even a single class of maladies. "Aspirin is a *panacea* for all headaches" is not the right way to use this word. While "Aspirin is a *panacea* for all ills" is better, it is still not perfect, because it is redundant. If a *panacea* is a cure for all ills, all you need to say is "Aspirin is a *panacea*."

pandemic / endemic / epidemic

See *epidemic / endemic / pandemic*.

paradigm / paragon -3 VOQ

Both of these words signify a *model*; however, a *paragon* is a model or exemplar of excellence, perfection, or lofty moral rectitude, as in "*paragon* of virtue," whereas a *paradigm* is, more neutrally, an example that serves as a model or to establish a pattern. Strictly speaking, only a person can be a *paragon*, while almost anything can be a *paradigm*. Be aware that *paradigm* has been overused of late by writers who specialize in trend spotting and forecasting, especially in business. The word, like fish kept more than three days, is beginning to stink. Use it sparingly, substituting *model* or *pattern* for the sake of variety.

parameters -2.5 VOQ

Parameters is in vogue as a synonym for boundaries or limits: "Running this unit faster than 2,000 rpm exceeds the recommended operating *parameters*." Many authorities object to what they consider the misappropriation of this term from mathematics, where it refers to constants in an equation or a set of independent variables. Even if you do accept the borrowing from mathematics, be aware that the use of the word has become a cliché and an instance of inflated diction.

pardon / reprieve

See *reprieve / pardon*.

parliamentarian -3 VOQ

Those elected to the British House of Commons are "members of Parliament," not *parliamentarians*, except for those members who happen also to be experts on parliamentary practice and rules of procedure. For that is what a *parlia-mentarian* is.

partake / participate   -2 VOQ

Avoid using *partake* where *participate* would serve better. To *partake* means primarily to take a share in or of with others: "I *partook* of dinner with the others." To take part in is better conveyed by *participate*: "I *participated* in the seminar," rather than "I *partook of* the seminar."

partially / partly   - 3 VOQ

Use *partially* to refer to incomplete things or things that have not reached fullness or some other extreme: "The sonata is only *partially* complete." Use *partly* in the sense of "in part," to refer to things that share features or characteristics with other things: "I am working on the sonata with another composer, so it is only *partly* mine."

party / person   -3 VOQ

Party is a legal term ("is a *party* to this agreement") and should be banished from everyday speech, in which it sounds just plain silly. Use *person* instead.

passed / past   -3 VOQ

Pronounced identically, these have different meanings. *Past* may function as an adjective, meaning no longer current, gone by, bygone, elapsed (in the *past* few minutes), or former (*past* president). It may also function as a noun, as in "the *past*" or "the judge's distinguished *past*." It may be a prep-osition, meaning beyond in time or in space ("He walked *past* my house because, so far as our affection is concerned, he is *past* that''); beyond in power, scope, extent, or influence (''The disease is *past* curing''); beyond in development (''That child should be *past* sucking his thumb!''); or beyond in terms of number or amount (''I tried eating more, but I couldn't get *past* my tenth burrito''). *Passed*, in contrast, has but one function, to be the *past* tense of the verb *pass*: ''He *passed* my house. That's right. He walked right *past* it.''

peaceable / peaceful   -3 VOQ

Peaceable people or animals are inclined to get along together and are disinclined to fight with one another. *Peaceful* people or animals are quiet, and a *peaceful* scene, setting, or environment is quiet and undisturbed.

pedal / peddle   -2 VOQ

To *pedal* is to pump the pedals of bicycle or use the pedals of a musical instrument, such as a piano or organ. To *peddle* is to sell, especially to travel from place to place selling small articles of merchandise.

pedant / pedagogue   -3 VOQ

Regrettably, these two words are often closely associated; however, they do have distinct meanings. A *pedant* is a person who revels in displaying a wealth of useless knowledge and who nitpicks and finds fault with the knowledge of others. ''She was a *pedant*, who repeatedly corrected my use of *shall* and *will*.'' *Pedagogue* is an inflated—and, indeed, *pedantic*—word for *teacher*.

penal / penile   -4 VOQ

This could be most embarrassing. Here are two adjectives,
one (*penal*) pertaining to punishment for crimes and offenses,
the other (*penile*) pertaining to the penis. Don't mix them
up.

penultimate   -3.5 VOQ

This word is very commonly and very annoyingly misused
as a synonym for *ultimate*, in the sense of the greatest or the
best: "He was an arrogant painter, thinking of himself as the
penultimate artist of our times." Actually, the primary meaning of *ultimate* is last or final, and the *only* legitimate
meaning of *penultimate* is second-to-last or next-to-final.

people / persons   -2 VOQ

A spurious rule of usage holds that *people* can never be preceded by a number. Don't say "ten *people*," but "ten *persons*." By extension, the "rule" dictates the use of *persons*
whenever a limited number is intended: "a few *persons*."

In truth, the only applicable rule here is what your ear tells
you. Sometimes *people* sounds more natural than *persons*
and vice versa. In general, you are on safe ground if you use
people when referring to *people* in general or to large groups
of unspecified number. *Persons* should be reserved for reference to small numbers and to exact numbers; however,
even in these cases, *people* will often do nicely as well.

per / as per   -4 VOQ

Per is a handy word when used in the sense of "for each":
"Rations are two biscuits *per* person." Regrettably, this

pleasant little word has been badly abused, especially in the
world of commerce: "*Per* your request, I am sending the
shipment overnight." This is a crude use of the word. Add
as, and you achieve illiteracy: "I have sent the shipment
overnight, *as per* your request." Just say "as you re-
quested."

perigee / apogee

See *apogee / perigee*.

persecute / prosecute -4 VOQ

Per- and *pro-* words all too readily create confusion. To *per-
secute* is continually to harass, hound, bother, oppress, or
harm someone. To *prosecute* may mean to carry out—"to
prosecute a project"—but it is most often used in the sense
of "press legal charges against": "I warn you, I am willing
to *prosecute* you in a court of law."

personal friend -2 VOQ

This is redundant, as is the phrase *close personal friend*.
Friendship is personal by definition and by its nature.

personnel -3 VOQ

Use this word only as a collective noun, not in reference to
individuals. "The saloon is frequented by military *personnel*
from the base" is fine, but "Four military *personnel* sat at
the bar" is incorrect. Substitute "four soldiers."

perspective / prospective   -4 VOQ

Another *per-* and *pro-* problem. *Perspective* refers to point
of view, whether literal, referring to the sense of sight, or
figurative, referring to intellectual or emotional inclinations:
"It is difficult to see the matter from his *perspective*." *Prospective* means potential or under consideration: "We inter-
viewed three *prospective* employees."

persuade / convince

See *convince / persuade*.

Peter Principle / Parkinson's Law / Murphy's Law

See *Murphy's Law / Peter Principle / Parkinson's Law*.

physical / fiscal

See *fiscal / physical*.

physician / doctor

See *doctor / physician*.

pier / dock / wharf

See *dock / pier / wharf*.

pinch hitter   -3 VOQ

This is not only a cliché but a universally misused cliché at
that! In baseball, a *pinch hitter* is not a second-best substitute,
but a batter the coach believes can perform more effectively

under the circumstances. In general use, however, *pinch hitter* signifies a substitute, not someone who is expected to do a better job.

piteous / pitiful -4 VOQ

Remarkably enough, these words, so often confused with each other, have opposite meanings. A *piteous* person deserves our compassion, whereas a *pitiful* one deserves our contempt. Both words may be applied to people, animals, events, or scenes. *Pitiful* may also be applied to an attempt to do or accomplish something: "He made a *pitiful* attempt to complete the project."

pivotal -2.5 VOQ

There is nothing wrong with this word, provided that it is used to mean something on which an issue or event turns: "The senator's vote was *pivotal*. On him, passage or failure of the bill depended." *Pivotal* is not synonymous with *important*. "Abortion is a *pivotal* issue" may be an accurate statement in some contexts, whereas "Abortion is an *important* issue" is accurate in all contexts.

plan ahead -3 VOQ

A tedious redundancy. How else can one *plan* other than *ahead*?

plan on / plan to -2 VOQ

Constructions using *plan on* are acceptable in most informal situations; however, the preferred preposition is *to*: "Do you *plan on* attending?" "I *plan to* attend."

playwright / playwrite / playwrighting / playwriting
-3 VOQ

A *playwright* writes plays, to be sure, but there is no such thing as a *playwrite*. The word is *playwright*, rooted (like *shipwright* and *wheelwright*) in *wright*, meaning a person who builds or repairs something. The implication of *playwright* is profound, suggesting that the art of creating a drama resembles, say, building a house more than writing a poem or other literary composition. This said, however, we must now observe that there is no such profession as *playwrighting*. The correct term is *playwriting*. No one ever gave the English language high marks for consistency.

plurality / majority

See *majority / plurality*.

plus
-4 VOQ

Plus is not the equivalent of *and*. *Plus* is a preposition meaning "with the addition of," whereas *and* is a conjunction. "He sold me this watch *plus* this wallet" is semiliterate English at best. Use *and*.

poor / pore / pour
-2 VOQ

This is a troublesome trio. *Poor* means impoverished, of low quality, or generally faulty. *Pore* may be a noun, meaning a minute opening in a tissue (as in a *pore* in the human skin) or a space in rock or soil that allows for the passage or absorption of water, or *pore* may be a verb, meaning to study intensively (*pore* over a book) or meditate deeply (to *pore* on the problem). *Pour* is a verb, meaning to flow in a continuous stream or to tip a container of fluid in order to transfer its contents from the container to another container or something else.

pornographic / obscene

See *obscene / pornographic*.

port / harbor

See *harbor / port*.

portable / mobile / movable

See *mobile / movable / portable*.

poser / poseur   -2.5 VOQ

You don't come across *poser* frequently, but if you did, it would properly mean a person who poses. Colloquially, a *poser* is also a puzzle, riddle, or conundrum. *Poseur* is more commonly encountered and means an affected, insincere person, who puts on airs and pretends to be something he is not.

preceding / previous   -2 VOQ

Don't mix these indiscriminately. *Preceding* means immediately before. "Look for that on the *preceding* page" means that, if you are on page 234, you'll find what you're looking for on page 233. *Previous* means anything that came before, not necessarily immediately before. Moreover, the word generally implies that the *previous* condition or circumstance no longer exists, applies, or has authority: "This law supersedes all *previous* opinions on the subject."

precipitant / precipitate / precipitation / precipitous / percipient
-3 VOQ

Let's take on these troublemakers one at a time. As an adjective, *precipitant* describes an action marked by impulsiveness or by a headlong rushing or falling. It may also be synonymous with *sudden* or *unexpected*. In chemistry, the word functions as a noun and describes a substance that causes the formation of a *precipitate* when it is added to a solution. *Precipitate* may function as an adjective synonymous with *precipitant*. When it does, it is pronounced "pre-SIP-uh-tit." However, *precipitate* is also much more. As a verb—in which form it is pronounced "pre-SIP-i-tate"—it may mean to throw or hurl from a lofty height: "The rock slipped, *precipitating* the travelers into the gorge below." Also as a verb, *precipitate* may mean to cause to happen: "His accident *precipitated* a lawsuit." Meteorologists use the word to describe what happens when water vapor condenses and falls as rain, snow, sleet, or hail: "If my prediction is correct, it will *precipitate* tomorrow." The resulting products—rain, snow, sleet, and hail—are encompassed by the noun *precipitation,* which, we shall see in a moment, has additional meanings as well. *Precipitate*, as a verb, serves the chemist to describe the process of separating a solid substance from a solution, thereby producing a *precipitate* (noun); the *precipitant* is the substance that brought about the separation of the *precipitate* from the solution.

Precipitation, we've just seen, is rain, sleet, snow, or hail. It is also a headlong fall or rush, impulsive haste, a hastening or acceleration. To the chemist, *precipitation* is the process of creating a *precipitant*.

Precipitous, all authorities agree, means extremely steep—that is, resembling a precipice. Some writers and speakers believe it is perfectly legitimate to use the word as a synonym for the adjective forms of *precipitant* and *precipitate*—that is, headlong, hasty, impulsive. Many others object to this usage of the word. Miss Nomer's opinion? With *precipitant* and *precipitate* handy, why select *precipitous*?

Now the odd man out in this group, *percipient*. This word is wholly unrelated to the others and describes someone who has especially keen powers of perception.

prejudice
-2.5 VOQ

A *prejudice* is a judgment formed in advance of the facts. It may be a judgment against or in favor of something. Typically, however, it is used in a strictly pejorative sense, to mean a destructive prejudgment against something or someone. This is not a misuse of the word, but it does neglect the word's full potential.

More serious is the careless use of *prejudice* to describe any position with which one doesn't happen to agree: "Sam has thought long and hard and has developed a *prejudice* against our product." By definition, *prejudice* is *pre*judgment and therefore cannot be the product of genuine judgment—that is, "long and hard" thought. It would seem that Sam doesn't have a *prejudice* against the product, but a poor opinion of it.

It is also sound practice to avoid using *prejudiced* without a clear referent, as in "Bill is *prejudiced*." A person is *prejudiced* for or against something or someone. Please specify against what or whom. Finally, avoid using *prejudiced*, without a referent, as a synonym for *bigoted*. If you wish to describe someone as a bigot, use *bigot*.

premeditated / deliberate

See *deliberate / premeditated.*

premier / premiere   **-3.5 VOQ**

Mistaking one for the other of these has punctured many a
pretentious bubble. *Premier* means number one, first in status
or rank. It may also function as a noun, as a label for the
chief administrative officer of certain nations or provinces.
A *premiere* is the first public performance of a play, a movie,
an opera, or a theatrical show. Although a few diehards protest that it can function legitimately only as a noun, *premiere*
is also generally used as a verb: "The play *premiered* to
great acclaim." *Premiere* may be spelled with an accent,
première, but this will be perceived as old-fashioned and
pretentious. Please take a look at *debut / premiere.*

premise / premises   **-4 VOQ**

If you are an urban dweller, doubtless you have seen signs
like this: Warning—This Premise Protected By Nabem Security Systems. Well, the protected area is only one residence
or business, so the singular *premise* seems appropriate.
Right?

Of course not.

In rhetoric and logic, a *premise* is a proposition on which
an argument is based. *Premises,* in this context, is plural:
more than one proposition. In the legal realm—and this includes matters of real estate—only the plural form, *premises*,
is correct. It describes a building or a parcel of land and the
buildings on that land. The insistence on the plural form is
not arbitrary, but a product of the word's history. It is derived
from the Medieval Latin *praemissa*, used in legal documents

from the Middle Ages and meaning "things mentioned before." In medieval property deeds, the items of property—land, house, outbuildings, and so on—were enumerated at the beginning of the document and, thereafter, referred to as *praemissa*: the "things mentioned before." Translated from the Latin into Old French and thence into Middle English as *premises*, the word has been applied to real property ever since.

present time, at the   -1.5 VOQ

This phrase comes in handy if you are getting paid for writing by the word, because it uses up a good many words. All that is necessary is *at present* or *now*. Also see *at this time*.

presume / assume

See *assume / presume*.

presumptive / presumptuous   -3.5 VOQ

Presumptive and *presumptuous* are different words with different meanings. The one cannot substitute for the other. *Presumptive* is principally a legal term used to designate something that is based on a presumption or that furnishes the basis for a supposition: "At this point, Mr. Johnson's involvement in the decision is *presumptive* only." *Presumptuous* is a term in general use, rather than peculiar to the legal profession, and is the equivalent of *arrogant*. It signifies the taking of excessive liberties or the *presumption* of too much: "It is *presumptuous* of you to assume that your election is a sure thing."

pretense / pretext   -2 VOQ

A most confusing pair! Think of *pretense* as the noun form
of *pretend*. It is make-believe, usually an act or a fiction
invented to hide one's true feelings. *Pretext* can be rather
more devious: an excuse, reason, or rationale put forth to
hide one's true purpose. It is a false front, an appearance
assumed intentionally to mislead: "His saying that he was
indifferent to her was a *pretense*. Actually, he was very much
in love with her and would find any *pretext*—such as re-
turning a borrowed book—to call on her."

primeval / primordial   -2 VOQ

Primeval pertains to the earliest ages of the world: "*Primeval* human beings lived a terrifying existence, but at least
they didn't have to contend with income tax." *Primordial*
reaches even further back, pertaining to what existed at the
very beginning or from the very beginning: "Unicellular organisms emerging from the *primordial* ooze did not lead ex-
citing lives, but at least they didn't have to contend with
income tax."

principal / principle   -4 VOQ

It is all too easy to mix these two up. *Principal* means first
in rank, authority, degree, or importance. It may be used as
an adjective or as a noun; thus the person called a headmaster
in private schools is called a *principal* in public schools, and
the major stockholders of a company or those in charge are
called the *principals*. *Principle* functions exclusively as a
noun and is synonymous with fundamental truth, prime doctrine, or intellectual or moral foundation.

prior to -1.5 VOQ

Why not just say *before*?

proceed -1.5 VOQ

Why not just say *go*? Or *walk, ride, drive,* and so on? Note also that *proceed* means "to move forward"; therefore, one cannot "*proceed* to back out" or "*proceed* to go backward."

progenitor -3.5 VOQ

Often misused in the sense of creator, originator, inventor, or father, *progenitor* is really a forefather or ancestor. "Guglielmo Marconi is credited as the *inventor* of radio, which is the *progenitor* of television."

prophecy / prophesy -3 VOQ

No, these aren't variant spellings; they are a noun and a verb. A *prophecy* is a prediction, while to *prophesy* is to predict. The *y* in the noun is pronounced like the *ee* in *seem*; in the verb, the *y* is pronounced like *eye*.

propitious / propitiate / auspicious

See *auspicious / propitious / propitiate*.

proportional / proportionate -2 VOQ

Use *proportional* to describe a relation between or among related elements: "The population of this city is *proportional* to the population of these others." Use *proportionate* to discuss the relationship of two different things: "The number of fleas is *proportionate* to the population of dogs."

proportions   -3 VOQ

Proportions is often used as a syllabically inflated synonym for size—"an aircraft of huge *proportions*"—but *proportions* expresses a relationship among parts. It does not signify absolute size. "With its short fuselage and oversize wings, the huge aircraft presented an odd set of *proportions*." If you feel the need for more than one syllable, use *dimensions* instead of *size*.

proposal / proposition   -1.5 VOQ

Used in the sense of a plan presented for acceptance, these two words are almost synonymous; however, their connotations diverge sufficiently to warrant care in their use. A *proposal* is a plan that is proposed or is the act of proposing. In a business context, it suggests an offer, a statement of what one can do. In contrast, *proposition* is closer to *deal*, and it connotes a take-it-or-leave-it attitude. *Proposition* may be seen as a shade less savory than *proposal*. After all, *proposal* is used to denote an offer of marriage, but a *proposition* can mean a request for sexual favors. These connotations carry over into other applications of these words as well.

prostate / prostrate   -2.5 VOQ

Perhaps because we are more accustomed to saying *prostrate*—lying flat, prone, or stretched out, face down, in adoring worship—the word also crops up in place of *prostate*, which, in men, is a gland around the neck of the bladder and urethra. The *prostate* is a frequent target of cancer: *prostate* (not *prostrate*) cancer.

protagonist   -2 VOQ

A movie, novel, or play may have many characters, but, properly speaking, it will have only a single *protagonist*. The word is derived from the Greek *protos* (first) and *agonistes* (actor). The concept of "first" is an absolute. There can be only one. Do not, therefore, speak of one *protagonist* fighting another or kissing another or speaking to another. If a movie, novel, or play clearly has more than one leading character, avoid *protagonist* in favor of "main characters" or, in the case of a drama or film, "stars."

prototype / archetype   -2 VOQ

Prototype is frequently used in the narrow and specialized sense of a working example of a product that is built before full-scale production begins. "The *prototype* is completed. As soon as we've tested it and evaluated the results, we should be able to set a date for full production." It may also be used to mean any original type, form, model, or early example of something: "Elaborate box kites served as *prototypes* for the Wright brothers' first successful airplane."

Although *archetype* can also denote the original type or model, it is not a synonym for *prototype*. The domain of *archetype* is cultural, literary, historical, and psychological, while that of *prototype* is principally technological and, to a lesser degree, historical. Most importantly, while a *prototype* can be purposely created ("Ford built a *prototype* of the Model T before beginning production"), an *archetype* is usually a product of nature, of human nature, of cultural development, or of historical circumstance. It can never be used in the sense of a purposely created preproduction example of a product. Also see *archetype / archetypal / archetypical.*

proven   -1.5 VOQ

In American English, the past participle of *prove* is *proved*, not *proven*: "The truth of this proposition was *proved* years ago."

provided / providing   -2 VOQ

The good news is that *either* of these forms is acceptable to assert a stipulation or condition: "You are welcome to stay, *provided* (or *providing*) that you clean up after yourself." The bad news is that many traditionalists are nevertheless appalled by *providing* and insist on *provided*. To avoid giving offense, use *provided.*

psychiatrist / psychologist / psychoanalyst   -2 VOQ

As with *ophthalmologist / optometrist / optician*, this trio describes three different, albeit related, professions. A *psychiatrist* is a medical doctor who specializes in the study, treatment, and prevention of mental illness. A *psychologist* does not have a medical degree. Clinical *psychologists*, like *psychiatrists*, treat patients with a variety of mental illnesses, while other *psychologists* may specialize in different areas involving the study of human or animal behavior, mental processes, and the like, not necessarily related to mental disorder. Finally, a *psychoanalyst* is a person trained in psychoanalysis, a particular method of treating mental and emotional disorders, originally formulated by Sigmund Freud. The *psychoanalyst* may also be a *psychiatrist* (this is the usual case in the United States) or a *psychologist.*

psycho / psychopath -2 VOQ

Despite appearances, *psycho* should be regarded not as a shortened form of *psychopath* but as very informal slang for a deeply disturbed, frightening, weird, demonic, and obviously crazed person. *Psychopath* describes a very specific psychiatric condition: an antisocial personality disorder characterized by perverted, criminal, and amoral behavior. The *psychopath* is apparently unaffected by socially accepted notions of right and wrong.

punctilious / punctual -4 VOQ

Only one of these words has anything to do with being on time, and *punctilious* isn't the one. *Punctual* means on time. *Punctilious* means lavishing excessive attention on matters of etiquette and protocol.

pupil / student -1.75 VOQ

When do you use *pupil* and when *student*? A *pupil* attends an elementary or middle school. A *student* attends high school or college. You'll raise few eyebrows if you call a third grader a *student*, but call a college senior a *pupil* and scorn will be heaped upon you.

purposefully / purposely -2 VOQ

Purposely is encountered far more commonly than *purposefully* and means intentionally, by design, on purpose. *Purposefully* should be reserved for occasions requiring a much stronger word. It does not mean merely intentionally, but implies great or at least significant purpose, the intention of achieving a goal: ''Jim *purposely* did not tell me about the contest'' implies mild deviousness on Jim's part, whereas ''Jim *purposefully* did not tell me about the contest'' suggests more sinister intentions. While we're at it, please take a look at *deliberate / premeditated*.

Q

que / queue / cue

See *cue / que / queue*.

quintessence / essence / epitome   -2 VOQ

Fast and loose is how these three are too often used. Think of *quintessence* as an intensification of *essence*. *Essence* is the ultimate, most basic nature of a thing, an idea, or a person's character, and *quintessence* underscores this meaning, suggesting the purest nature of an entity. Be aware, however, that *essence* has a specific meaning in philosophy—as the individual, the real, or the ultimate nature of a thing, in contrast to that thing's existence, which is mutable—and *quintessence* cannot properly be used to intensify this meaning.

Epitome is frequently misused when *essence* or *quintessence* is called for, and vice versa. An *epitome* may be a summary or condensation or outline, but is more frequently used to mean a perfect example or ideal representative of a type or a class: ''Richard Nixon was, for better or worse, the *epitome* of an American politician.''

quote / quotation   -2.5 VOQ

Most conscientious writers and speakers would find this sentence objectionable: "The essay includes *quotes* from many famous politicians." The correct word here is *quotations*. Use *quote* as a verb and *quotation* as a noun.

R

rack / wrack   -3 VOQ

In the sense of ruin or destroy, these homonyms cause confusion. A *rack* is a frame, and, as a verb, may mean to torture or stretch, as on the medieval device called a *rack*, or, as *racked*, to be consumed with pain, misery, sobs, coughing, and so on. *Wrack* is derived from *wreck* and means to ruin or destroy. As a noun, it is usually coupled with *ruin* in the phrase *wrack and ruin*.

raise / rear   -1.5 VOQ

Most readers and listeners now accept the following: "This is how I intend to *raise* my children." However, a small but vocal corps of traditionalists continue to insist that one *raises* animals but *rears* children. If you wish absolutely to avoid giving offense, use *rear* rather than *raise*. (It should be observed, however, that few parents object to *raise*, no matter what their linguistic leanings. Whether linguistically liberal or conservative, most fathers and mothers agree that children are, in essence, animals.)

raise / rise -4 VOQ

These won't confuse you if you remember that *raise* is a transitive verb, which means that it must have an object, must act on something, whereas *rise* is intransitive and does not take an object. "I will *raise* the window" has the subject (I) doing something *to* the object (window). "The sun will *rise*" has a subject (sun) and verb only—no object.

rare / scarce -3.5 VOQ

A shade of meaning separates *rare* from *scarce*. *Rare* items are difficult to obtain, expensive, and valuable: "Diamonds are *rare*." *Scarce* items are in short supply, but often only temporarily, and may or may not be of significant intrinsic value: "During the long drought, supplies of fresh water became *scarce*."

ravage / ravish -3.5 VOQ

These two are often confused with each other. Result: embarrassing comedy. To *ravage* is to destroy. To *ravish* is to overwhelm with emotion, to seize passionately, or to rape—though, in this last sense, *ravish* is decidedly archaic and should be avoided.

ravel / unravel -0 VOQ

Both of these denote coming apart, whether it is the hem of a garment, the tangled web of a mystery as it is solved, or the structure of a failing business deal. All speakers, writers, listeners, and readers should find both words equally acceptable; however, see *loosen / unloosen*, where you'll discover that *unloosen* does not enjoy the same degree of acceptance as *unravel*.

readable / legible   -3 VOQ

Writing is *readable* when the thoughts it embodies are clearly and vigorously expressed, thereby stimulating the reader, who is motivated to read on. *Readability* is a product of the writer's skill and the nature of his or her subject. Writing is *legible* when the letters on the page are sufficiently large, clear, dark, and neatly formed to be readily intelligible without confusion. *Legibility* is the product of the writer's penmanship or the printer's skill; it is a function of the physical appearance of the words, letters, and the medium on which these are inscribed.

reason is because   -4 VOQ

"The *reason* for her early departure *is because* of a dental appointment." This all too common construction is redundant, clunky, and just plain wrong. *Because* means *for the reason that*, so you hardly need to add the word *reason*. Either say "The *reason* for her early departure is a dental appointment" or "She left early *because* of a dental appointment."

rebut / refute   -3.5 VOQ

To *rebut* is to argue the contrary of a statement or position; to *refute* is to argue this definitively and successfully: "If you *rebut* this article skillfully, you will *refute* the organization's argument." Also see *confute / refute*.

recant / retract   -3 VOQ

Recant and *retract* both refer to changing or withdrawing an official statement. Of the two, *recant* is the stronger, signifying a disavowal of a former position and an admission that the statement and the position that motivated it were wrong. To *retract* is formally to withdraw or alter a statement, but not necessarily to admit a fundamental error in the basis or position from which the statement was made.

rectitude / turpitude

See *turpitude / rectitude*.

recur / reoccur   -1 VOQ

Both of these words are real. Feel free to use either. They are differentiated by a shade of meaning. *Recur* implies repeated or even cyclical repetition. *Reoccur* implies onetime repetition: "We decided that the safety inspections should *recur* on a fixed schedule to help prevent a *reoccurrence* of the accident."

reformed alcoholic   -4 VOQ

Medical authorities agree that alcoholism is a disease. So far, it has proved incurable, though treatable: one can stop drinking. But since alcoholism is a disease rather than a moral failing, *reformed alcoholic* is both inaccurate and offensive. Use *recovering alcoholic* instead to describe an alcoholic who has stopped drinking.

refute / confute

See *confute / refute*.

regardless
-3 VOQ

This word always needs the assistance of the preposition *of*: "*Regardless of* your political beliefs, you are welcome here." Also see *irregardless*.

regime
-3 VOQ

This word is properly reserved for denoting a system of rule, not the administration of a particular individual. Thus it is correct to refer to the former Soviet Union's Communist *regime*, but it is not correct to speak of the *regime* of Joseph Stalin, although many people spoke and wrote of it in just this way.

reluctant / reticent
-3 VOQ

Reluctant is almost never misused. It means unwilling or at least not eager. *Reticent* is often carelessly used as synonym for *reluctant*: "George was *reticent* about starting the job." To be *reticent* is to be *reluctant—reluctant* to speak. A *reticent* person is quiet, a man or woman of few words. Thus *reticent* may be used to describe a general characteristic; however, it may also be applied to a specific instance: "He was *reticent* about his role in the project."

repeat again
-3 VOQ

Another flash from the Department of Redundancy Department. To *repeat again* is to *repeat*. Period.

repel / repulse   -2 VOQ

"You *repulse* me!" Presumably the speaker means to express her disgust, but her sentence means "You push me away." The word she wants is *repel*, which may mean to drive off *or* to disgust. Reserve *repulse* for use in the sense of drive off or push away: "The Union forces successfully *repulsed* Pickett's charge."

repertoire / repertory   -1 VOQ

These words are not entirely interchangeable. *Repertoire* is the store of plays, songs, dance routines, musical pieces, or other selections a performer or performing company has at its command. Outside of a performing context, the word may be used to denote the range of skills or abilities a person or organization possesses: "My *repertoire*, Mr. Perkins, includes everything from wholesale to retail sales." While *repertory* may be used as an Anglicized synonym for *repertoire*, its preferred meaning is a theater or theatrical company that performs works from a specifically defined *repertoire*. In this sense, the word can be used alone as a noun ("Let's buy tickets to the *repertory* tonight") or as an adjective with another noun: "He acted in the *repertory* company."

repetitious / repetitive   -2 VOQ

Repetitive is applied to an action or activity that happens over and over. *Repetitious* is applied to a person who habitually repeats himself. The word may also be applied to a piece of music or writing that tends to repeat the same or similar material in a tedious manner.

replete / complete

See *complete / replete*.

replica   -1.5 VOQ

Don't treat *replica* as if it were a synonym for *copy, repro-
duction,* or *model.* Properly used, *replica* applies only to an
exact copy of an original. In its very strictest sense, a *replica*
is a copy made by the original creator or artist.

repress / suppress / oppress

See *oppress / repress / suppress*.

reprieve / pardon   -3 VOQ

A *reprieve* is a postponement of judicial punishment or other
unpleasant consequences of some action. It may also be used
as a near-synonym for *relief*: "I need a *reprieve* from this
continual drudgery." In legal terms, a *reprieve* may result in
the cancellation of punishment, but the connotation of the
word is first and foremost temporary: a postponement. In
contrast, a *pardon* is permanent. Issued by an official with
appropriate authority, such as a governor or the president of
the United States, it cancels all punishment for a specific
crime.

reprisal / reprise   -4 VOQ

A *reprise,* pronounced "re-PREEZ," is the repetition of a
melody, musical phrase, or song: "The melody is heard at
the beginning of Act I and then is heard, as a *reprise*, in Act
III." The word may also be used as a verb: "The melody

heard in Act I is *reprised* in Act III." A *reprise* may also be a repeat performance: "The appearance was a *reprise* of his earlier performance." A *reprisal* is retaliation: "He insulted his boss repeatedly and, by way of *reprisal*, was refused a promotion."

reputation / character

See *character / reputation*.

resister / resistor   -2 VOQ

A person who opposes an action or who defies and withstands the imposition of some decree, law, or other action is a *resister*: "During the Vietnam War, many U.S. draft *resisters* fled to Canada." A *resistor* is not a human being, but an electric or electronic device that functions to introduce resistance into an electrical circuit.

restauranteur   -4 VOQ

This singularly irritating misspelling and mispronunciation of *restaurateur* will strip hard-earned stars from the rating of anyone who writes or utters it. As with so many dining terms, the word was taken directly from the French, who left out the *n* and did not give us leave to put it back in. The person who owns or runs a restaurant is a *restaurateur*.

restive / restful   -4 VOQ

Two more examples of how many English words sound alike, yet mean opposite, or very nearly opposite, things. To be *restive* is to be restless. *Restful*, of course, means peaceful, relaxed, or conducive to relaxation and tranquillity.

return back -3 VOQ

Shun this clumsy redundancy. *Return*, unaided by another word, is adequate to the job.

revenge / avenge

See *avenge / revenge*.

reverend -3 VOQ

Reverend is never properly used as a noun. "I spoke to the *reverend* this morning" is incorrect English and may even be perceived as gauche. As an honorific title, *Reverend* is capitalized and always preceded by *the*. It should not be used with the clergyman's last name only, but either with his or her full name or with another title: "the Reverend George Johnson" or "the Reverend Dr. Johnson." If you remember that *reverend* is an adjective, you won't render it as a plural: "the Reverends John Smith and Sarah Jones." Use "the Reverend John Smith and the Reverend Sarah Jones" or the abbreviation "Rev.": "Rev. John Smith and Rev. Sarah Jones." Note that when the abbreviation is used, *the* is not necessary.

reverse / converse

See *converse / reverse*.

revert back -3.5 VOQ

Like *return back*, *revert back* is redundant. If one *reverts*, *back* is the only available direction.

review / revue   -2 VOQ

A *review* is an evaluation, an examination, a study, or a reevaluation or reexamination—in effect a re-view, a second look at something or some body of knowledge. The word can also be used as a verb: ''Please *review* the material and discuss it with me.'' *Revue* is used only as a noun and is a theatrical presentation consisting of skits, songs, and dances rather than a unified narrative story.

rifle / riffle   -2 VOQ

As a noun, *rifle* is a long firearm with a characteristically rifled bore. As a verb, the word means to ransack and plunder. Add another *f* and the word becomes kinder, gentler, describing the action of leafing rapidly through a book. ''The thief, a desperate college graduate, *rifled* the house, then paused to *riffle* the pages of a book he had stolen.'' Also see *gun / rifle*.

rob   -3 VOQ

To *rob* means to steal from: ''He will *rob* the bank'' means he will steal from the bank. ''He *robbed* the money'' is poor English (he will rob from the money?). Avoid prosecution for illiteracy by using *rob* only in the sense of *steal from*. Also see *burglar / robber / thief*.

robber / thief / burglar

See *burglar / robber / thief*.

S

saber / sabre   -2 VOQ

The *saber* is a venerable, even archaic, weapon, which may tempt you to apply to it the esoteric-looking British *-re* spelling. Don't yield to temptation, at least not in the U.S.A. We spell it *saber*.

sachet / sashay   -2 VOQ

Sachet, a noun, is a little packet of perfumed powder used to scent clothes that are stored in closets, drawers, or trunks. *Sashay*, a verb, denotes either an exaggeratedly casual style of walking or a strutting, flouncing gait. A variant of *chassé*, the word also denotes a sidestep in dance.

safe / vault

See *vault / safe*.

sake / saki   -2 VOQ

Sushi is *sushi*, not *sushe*, but it does not follow that *sake* is *saki*. It is most commonly spelled *sake*.

salable / saleable   -2 VOQ

Like other words ending in *-able*, *salable* drops the silent *e* in the first part of the compound.

salutatorian / valetudinarian / valedictorian

See *valedictorian / salutatorian / valetudinarian*.

sanitarium / sanitorium   -1 VOQ

You won't get in much trouble if you use these two inter-changeably. *Sanitarium*, the more often used word, signifies a hospital, usually dedicated to the treatment of patients with long-term physical and mental disorders. *Sanitorium*, a some-what outmoded term, suggests an institution that is more of a health resort or spa than a hospital.

savings   -2.5 VOQ

"If you buy now, the widget will cost you only $150—a *savings* of five dollars!" This is not only a questionable bar-gain but a semiliterate sentence to boot. The noun is singular here and should be used as such: "a *saving* of five dollars."

scarce / rare

See *rare / scarce*.

Scotch / Scottish   -2 VOQ

Scotch is whisky—the Scots spell it without the *e*. *Scotch* should not be used as an adjective describing a person from Scotland. Use *Scottish* instead. (Some authorities hold that *Scotch* may be safely used as an adjective to describe things, while *Scottish* should always be used to describe people. Maybe. But why not take the safest course? Use *Scottish* whenever you need an adjective.)

scrutiny   -2 VOQ

Scrutiny is a word that attracts redundancy as a magnet draws iron filings. By definition, *scrutiny* is minute, painstakingly close inspection; therefore, the familiar phrases *close scrutiny* and *careful scrutiny* are wastefully redundant and should be reduced to *scrutiny* alone.

sculpt   -3 VOQ

The snooty and the snobby have no qualms about using *sculpt*, but that doesn't make it a good word. Like most back-formations, *sculpt* (from *sculpture*) is awkward and of doubtful legitimacy. Use *sculpture* as a verb as well as a noun, and let *sculpt* wither and die.

seasonable / seasonal   -3 VOQ

Something is *seasonable* if it is appropriate to the season, as warm, muggy weather is *seasonable* in August. Something is *seasonal* if it is connected with seasons: "These resort rates are subject to a *seasonal* increase beginning on June 15."

secede / cede

See *cede / secede*.

seize / siege   -3 VOQ

Seize is a verb, meaning to take, especially by force. *Siege* is a noun describing a military blockade of a city or fortress with the object of *seizing* it. Note that *seize* violates the customary *i*-before-*e*-except-after-*c* spelling rule, but that *siege* obeys the rule.

self-confessed   -4 VOQ

To confess is to admit and proclaim one's culpability. You cannot confess by proxy; therefore, confession is by definition self-confession, which makes the *self-* part redundant. Kill it and bury it.

semi- / bi-

See *bi- / semi-*.

sensual / sensuous   -2 VOQ

Both words pertain to the senses, but *sensual* implies gratification or indulgence of the physical appetites, especially the sexual appetites, whereas *sensuous* suggests aesthetic pleasure. There is, however, a good deal of overlap between the two words.

service   -5 VOQ

The indiscriminate use of *service* as a verb in place of *serve* is unintentionally hilarious and bawdy: "Did anyone *service* you yet?" This is very distracting and, though sometimes good for laughs, sufficiently disruptive of effective communications to warrant a -5 VOQ. The only correct verb is *serve*, not *service*, except when the meaning is "perform maintenance or repair": "The mechanic *serviced* the engine."

set / sit -4 VOQ

To *set* is to put or place: "Set that vase there, please." To *sit* is to take a seated position: "Sit there, please." Note that *set* is a transitive verb and must have an object ("that vase"), while *sit* is intransitive and takes no object. Mixing up *set* and *sit* will be perceived as a literacy problem, unless you are a country music singer.

sewage / sewerage -3 VOQ

The word *sewage* is rarely misused, while *sewerage* is rarely used at all. No, it is not a misspelling of *sewage. Sewage* is the effluvia—waste matter and excess water—and *sewerage* is the system of sewers through which the *sewage* passes.

sex / gender

See *gender / sex.*

shall / will -1.5 VOQ

The distinction between these two used to seem important, but it has now faded into insignificance. To express simple futurity, we were supposed to use *shall* with the first person and *will* with the second and third. However, to express determination, permission, compulsion, or obligation, we were supposed to remember to use *shall* with the second and third persons and *will* with the first. In most cases, *will* has simply supplanted *shall,* regardless of person or circumstance. *Shall* is still used to lend an air of formality to certain expressions, and it is the only choice in some questions, such as "*Shall* we go?"

shear / sheer   -3 VOQ

These are troublesome homonyms. *Shear* means to cut ("use
an electric razor to *shear* the sheep"), and *sheer* can mean
very thin, almost transparent ("*sheer* stockings"), or almost
perpendicular ("a *sheer* drop of a thousand feet"). *Sheer* has
an additional meaning as a verb—to *swerve*: "Our plane
sheered sharply left."

ship / boat

See *boat / ship*.

should of   -5 VOQ

An illiteracy. The correct phrase is *should have* or the contraction *should've*.

[*sic*]   -4 VOQ

This little piece of Latin—it means "thus"—litters academic
writing. It is properly used to indicate awareness of an error
in quoted material, so that the reader does not think the material has been misquoted: "Bill Clinton is the precedent [*sic*]
of the United States." "[*sic*]" is often improperly used to
elbow the reader in the ribs, lest he fail to get a joke or pun:
"We sell sexy used cars and other auto-erotica [*sic*]." It is
also often overused, for example to mark every misspelling
in a quotation that includes many misspellings.

Use "[*sic*]"—in brackets and with italics—only when
there is genuine danger that a reader will doubt the accuracy
of a quotation.

silicon / silicone
-3 VOQ

Next to oxygen, *silicon* is the most abundant element in the earth's crust. Nevertheless, few people gave it much thought until it became widely used in the manufacture of semiconductor chips for computers and other electronic devices. *Silicone*, a compound derived from *silicon*, is widely used as a lubricant. It is also used in the manufacture of highly elastic rubber. Just as few people cared much about *silicon* before the advent of the personal computer, so few gave much thought to *silicone* until *silicone* rubber appeared as a prosthetic device to enlarge the breasts. If you still have trouble knowing when to use *silicon* and when to use *silicone*, remember that the area centered on San Jose, California, has been dubbed Silicon Valley because so much of the electronics industry is located there. For the breast implant capital, you should look down the coast, to Beverly Hills, which you may think of as Silicone Valley.

since / because

See *because / since*.

sinus
-4 VOQ

"I have terrible *sinus* this spring." Too bad. If your *sinusitis* is as bad as your English, you must indeed be suffering. *Sinus* is not a disorder but a cavity in tissue or bone. The correct term is *sinusitis, sinus trouble,* or *sinus condition*.

skirt around
-3 VOQ

To *skirt* is to detour or move around; therefore, the *around* is redundant. Jettison it.

slander / liable / libel

See *liable / libel / slander*.

## snuck	-4 VOQ

Snuck is illiterate and must be shunned. The correct past tense of *sneak* is *sneaked*.

sofa / couch / davenport / divan

See *couch / davenport / divan / sofa*.

## sometime, some time	-3 VOQ

When do you make this one word? When two? If you want to express an indefinite point in time, use *sometime*: "We will get the results *sometime* next week." If you want to express an indefinite span of time, use *some time*: "I've been expecting those results for *some time* now."

## sooner . . . when	-4 VOQ

Everybody knows that *than* follows the comparative *sooner*: "Bill arrived *sooner than* expected." Yet this construction is also quite common: "No *sooner* did I buy the new computer *when* it went on sale for less." Quite common—and quite wrong. *Sooner . . . when*? Miss Nomer thinks not. Even if other words follow *sooner*, this comparative calls for *than* and only *than*.

special / especial

See *especial / special*.

spell out
-2 VOQ

"Let me *spell out* the repayment terms for you . . ." In the sense of specify and explain the details, *spell out* is a rather tired phrase, and you may wish to avoid it for this reason. In any case, do avoid *spell out the details*, since to *spell out* is to do just that. Don't heap redundancy on top of a cliché.

spiraling
-2 VOQ

"Costs are *spiraling* out of control." Yes, but in which direction? This word requires qualification upward or downward: "Costs are *spiraling* up out of control, while profits continue to *spiral* downward."

stalactite / stalagmite
-3 VOQ

Spelunkers would rate misuse of these at -5 VOQ. *Stalactites* are conical mineral formations found in caves. They hang down from the ceiling of the cave. *Stalagmites* are also cone-shaped mineral formations, but they rise from the cave floor. *Stalactites* down from the top; *stalagmites* up from the bottom.

stalemate
-2 VOQ

As every chess player knows, a *stalemate* is forever. It is not a temporary impasse that can be resolved through negotiation. It is the end of the game. Take care, then, how you use *stalemate* figuratively. If you wish to express a dead end, *stalemate* is your word. If, however, negotiations are merely stalled or have suffered a temporary setback, find a more appropriate term, such as *obstacle* or *roadblock*.

stationary / stationery   -2 VOQ

If a thing is *stationary*, it is standing still. If a thing is *stationery*, it is intended to be written on.

staunch / stanch   -1 VOQ

Staunch, an adjective means firm or steadfast; it can also mean strong, substantially constructed, or substantially constituted. *Stanch* means to stop or check the flow of some liquid, usually blood and sometimes tears. If you suffer an accident and cut yourself, better find a *staunch* friend to help you *stanch* the flow of blood. *Stanch* may also be used figuratively: ''I took a scissors to all my credit cards in order to *stanch* the flow of cash from my bank account.''

Probably because the word *stanch* looks like a misspelling of *staunch*, the latter is often misused for the verb meaning to stop the flow. It's been misused so often that some dictionaries have thrown in the towel (handy for *stanching* purposes, by the way) and now permit *staunch* to serve as verb as well as adjective. For that reason—and that reason alone—this blunder rates only a -1 VOQ. Note, however, that while you might get by substituting *staunch* for *stanch*, you cannot use *stanch* for *staunch*. Even your *staunchest* friends will desert you if you call them your *stanch* friends.

sterile / antiseptic   -2.5 VOQ

A *sterile* substance is free from bacteria and all other living things. A *sterile* organism cannot produce offspring. *Sterile* land is barren. A *sterile* mind is barren of ideas. All of these meanings differ significantly from *antiseptic*, which, as an adjective or as a noun, pertains to substances that inhibit or prevent the growth of bacteria. Note, however, that both *ster-*

ile and *antiseptic* can be used figuratively; *sterile* always suggests barrenness, while *antiseptic* suggests a disagreeable degree of fastidiousness: "The politician didn't wish to offend anyone, and his remarks struck me as *antiseptic*."

stevedore / longshoreman

See *longshoreman / stevedore*.

straight / strait   -4 VOQ

Straight is the opposite of crooked, but *strait* means tight and confining. A violent lunatic is put in a *straitjacket*, not a straight jacket, because he needs confinement, not an improvement in posture. A person who has exceeded her credit limit is said to be in *straitened* circumstances, because her financial situation is tight and confining. She is obliged to *straighten* out her financial affairs. Unlike *straight, strait* can serve as a noun as well as an adjective. A *strait* is a narrow channel joining two larger bodies of water; it is often used as a plural: *straits*. A metaphoric extension of this geographical meaning is *strait* or *straits* in the sense of a difficult situation: "The loss of his job put Pete in dire *straits* (or a dire *strait*)."

strangled to death   -3.5 VOQ

How else would one be *strangled*? "The victim was found *strangled*" means the victim was found dead. *Strangled to death* is overkill.

strata / stratum   -3 VOQ

One of many words our language has borrowed from Latin,
strata / stratum is among the few that retain their original
Latin singular and plural. *Strata* is plural, which means that
"He rose to a higher social *strata*" is wrong. Use the singular, *stratum,* or, better yet, plain old *level*. But "He rose
through the various social *strata*" is correct.

strategy / stratagem   -3 VOQ

Strategy is the art and science of planning and conducting
war or other usually massive enterprises, such as running a
large corporation. A *stratagem* is a plan or scheme or trick
for deceiving or surprising an enemy. In a somewhat broader
sense, a *strategem* is any deception, clever maneuver, or con-
trivance. Successful *strategy* often includes the formulation
and deployment of clever *strategems*.

stringent / astringent / strident   -3.5 VOQ

Stringent is synonymous with *strict* in the sense of tightly
regulated and carefully controlled, as in "*stringent* require-
ments for admission to the program." *Astringent* pertains to
a substance that cleans the skin and constricts the pores. *Strident* is an adjective meaning loud, sharp, grating, and dis-
cordant. It is most often used figuratively to describe the
advocacy of ideological positions with which one does not
happen to agree, as in "She was a *strident* feminist."

subsequent to   -1.5 VOQ

Why not just use *after*? *Subsequent to* is pretentious and
wordy.

substitute with   -4 VOQ

"I will *substitute* whole milk *with* skim milk." Wrong—and confusing. Is this person going to use skim or whole milk? Fortunately, this is a simple error to avoid. *For* is the only preposition to use with *substitute*: "I will *substitute* skim milk for whole milk."

suit / suite   -2 VOQ

In some parts of the country, especially the South, these two word are often pronounced identically, as *suit*. This is not a good idea. A *suit* is a set of clothing meant to be worn together (typically consisting of pants or skirt and a matching jacket), a set of related playing cards, or the process of suing in a court of law, whereas a *suite*—pronounced "sweet"— is an ensemble, a number of things that form a set (as in a series of related musical pieces, like *The Nutcracker Suite)*, or a set of furniture, as in a bedroom *suite*.

suppress / oppress / repress

See *oppress / repress / suppress*.

surprise / astonish   -1.5 VOQ

These are not synonyms. To *surprise* is to say or do something unexpected. To *astonish* is to say or do something that causes wonder. While both words may imply wonderment, only *surprise* conveys the element of the unexpected.

susceptible / vulnerable   -2 VOQ

There is overlap between the appropriate venues for this pair, but they are hardly synonyms. To be *susceptible* is to be especially subject to some influence or agent, as in "George is *susceptible* to colds" or "Miss Nomer is not *susceptible* to flattery." To be *vulnerable* is to be exposed to possible damage or wounding; this may be physical, emotional, or moral: "The candidate, unable to explain his vast collection of ladies' footgear, was *vulnerable* to questions concerning his character."

suspected / accused / alleged

See *alleged / accused / suspected*.

swank / swanky   -3 VOQ

Many authorities object to both of these words as overly casual for formal discourse and even vulgar; however, if you must use one of them, choose *swank* and reject *swanky*, a word guaranteed to raise more eyebrows than *swank*.

T

take place / happen / occur   -2 VOQ

Many, perhaps most, speakers and writers use these three interchangeably; however, only *happen* and *occur* are fully interchangeable. They may be used to signify any event or occasion, but they imply that whatever happened was spontaneous, unplanned, or accidental. In contrast, *take place* implies a planned or scheduled event: "The wreck *occurred* yesterday at about three," but "The ceremony will *take place* tomorrow at exactly three."

tandem   -2 VOQ

In the days of the horse and carriage, this word would never have caused confusion. Everyone knew that horses hitched in *tandem* were one behind the other, in single file rather than side by side. Think of a *tandem* bicycle.

taps   -2 VOQ

Taps should be treated like *reveille*, since both are military bugle calls. Neither is the title of a musical composition, so no italics or quotation marks are called for. Nor should an initial capital be used. Note, too, that *taps* is singular and should be treated as such: "*Taps* was sounded."

taro / tarot   -2.5 VOQ

The New Age is more distinguished for its advocacy of crystals and homeopathy than for the unerring accuracy of its spelling. *Taro* is a plant cultivated, especially in the Pacific islands, for its fleshy edible tuber. *Tarot*, pronounced like *taro*, is a deck of twenty-two cards, each bearing an allegorical inscription and figure, used in telling fortunes.

tasteful / tasty   -2 VOQ

What is *tasty* is delicious. What is *tasteful* is characterized by good taste—that is, a discernment and decorousness unlikely to offend anyone.

teepee, tepee, tipi   -2.5 VOQ

All three spellings of this word have been used in print,
though *tipi* looks especially strange and is rarely used these
days. Some authorities reject *teepee* as well. *Tepee* is accepted by everyone.

telecast / telecasted   -3 VOQ

Like *broadcast*, *telecast* serves as both present and past
tense. *Telecasted* is not used.

temerity / timidity   -3.5 VOQ

Perhaps because it sounds rather like *timorous*, which describes a person or animal suffering from an excess of *timidity*, *temerity* is sometimes confused with *timidity*. It is, in
fact, the very opposite: presumptuousness or unwarranted
boldness. Here's an example: "After selling me this defective radio, how can you have the *temerity* to talk to me about
buying a television from you?"

temperature   -2.5 VOQ

"Baby has a *temperature*." No, the poor little thing has a
fever, or, if you wish to report the details, he has a "*temperature* of 101°F."

than / then   -5 VOQ

Perhaps it is an overabundance of lazy ears that accounts for
the great frequency with which these two very basic words
are misused. They do, after all, sound alike. *Than* is a conjunction used to introduce the second element of an unequal

comparison. An example will make this clear: "Bill is fatter *than* Tom." *Then* is usually an adverb meaning at that time ("I can meet you *then*"), next ("I washed the dishes and *then* took out the trash"), and in addition, besides, or moreover ("John is stupid, and *then* he's also ugly"). Besides these meanings, *then*, preceded by *but*, is used as a qualifier or a balancer: "He was successful, *but then* his daddy had given him a million dollars to start his business." *Then* may mean "in that case": "If you try it this way, *then* it will work." *Then* may mean *therefore*: "We are, *then*, agreed." The final adverbial meaning of *then* is "that time": "Let's work for another hour, *then* go to a saloon." *Then* may be used as an adjective, though this use has always seemed clunky to Miss Nomer: "I started the business with my *then* husband, Egbert." Note that *then*, used as an adjective, is not followed by a hyphen: *then*-husband.

Having explained the uses of *then*, let's return to *than*. Since it is considered a conjunction, the pronoun that follows it must be in the same case as the antecedent. Just look at this example: "He is more concerned about cost *than I*." *Than I*, not *than me*. *He* is in the nominative case, so *I* must also be. Fortunately, you don't have to be a grammarian to figure this out. Sentences like "He is more concerned *than I*" are called elliptical, because they leave something out: the second verb. If you add that second verb (in your mind), you won't get the pronoun wrong: "He is more concerned *than I am*." Your ear will not let you say "*me am*."

that / which -2.5 VOQ

There are rules—rational, meaningful rules—that govern the use of *that* and *which*. Let's take a look at them.

Consider these three sentences:

Cars *that* have flat tires don't get very far.

Cars *which* have flat tires don't get very far.

Cars, *which* have flat tires, don't get very far.

The first sentence is not only a true statement, it is also grammatically correct. The second certainly is grammatically incorrect and may or may not be false as well. (We cannot tell, because the grammatical error obscures the writer's intended meaning.) The third sentence is grammatically correct, but the statement is false.

"Cars *that* have flat tires don't get very far" means that only those cars with flat tires don't get very far—that is, the sentence tells us that not all cars have flat tires. Some do. Some don't. A car may have flat tires, but flat tires do not define a car. The phrase "*that* have flat tires" is called a restrictive clause, because it restricts the meaning of the sentence to a certain class (cars with flat tires). Restrictive clauses are always introduced by *that* (never *which*), and they are never set off with commas.

"Cars which have flat tires don't get very far" is an ambiguous sentence. Why? *Which* can be used only to introduce a nonrestrictive clause—a clause that defines and does not limit the subject of the sentence. Nonrestrictive clauses must be set off with commas. So we know this much about this sentence: it is grammatically incorrect. But does the writer mean that only cars with flat tires don't get very far? In this case, he should have used *that* instead of *which*. Or does he mean that all cars have flat tires—flat tires are a defining characteristic of cars—and that therefore no car gets very far? If that was his meaning, he should have written the third sentence: "Cars, *which* have flat tires, don't get very far." This is grammatically sound. The *which* introduces a nonrestrictive clause, which is set off by commas. Of course, grammatically correct or not, the sentence is a false statement. A car cannot be defined correctly as a vehicle with flat tires. But that is precisely what the third sentence does.

How do you know when to use a restrictive clause (introduced by *that* and not set off with commas) and when to use a nonrestrictive clause (introduced by *which* and set off with commas)? Ask yourself what would happen if you eliminated the clause. Would the sentence still convey the meaning you intend? Could it stand meaningfully without the clause? If we take out "*that* have flat tires," we are left with "Cars don't get very far." Obviously, this is not the meaning we intend. The sentence cannot stand meaningfully without the clause; therefore, the clause is restrictive, must be introduced by *that*, and must not be set off with commas. Contrast this sentence: "Cars, *which* have four wheels, are a popular form of transportation." Eliminate the clause "*which* have four wheels," and the sentence still makes good sense: "Cars are a popular form of transportation." The clause adds meaning to the sentence, but it is not essential to the basic meaning of the sentence. It is therefore nonrestrictive and must be introduced by *which* and set off with commas.

that which   -2 VOQ

The phrase *that which* can usually be discarded in favor of the more economical and less pretentious *what*. "*That which* is used develops; *that which* is not used atrophies." This could be better expressed with *what*: "*What* is used develops; *what* is not used atrophies."

their / there / they're   -4 VOQ

A mix-up among these is characteristically laughed off as a mere slip of the pen or word processor. The fact is, the writer who misuses these runs the risk of being judged stupid and thereby sabotaging his message. *Their* is the possessive form of *they*: "I wrote down *their* names." *There* is a Swiss army knife among words, meaning at or in that place ("I'll sit over *there*"), to or toward ("I wouldn't go *there* if I were you"), at that point or moment ("Stop right *there* before you make a fool of yourself"), and in that matter ("I agree with you *there*"). *There* can also introduce a clause or a sentence: "*There* used to be fish in this pond." *There* can be used to indicate an unspecified person in a phrase such as "Hello *there*." It can be used as an intensive: "Talk to that person *there* about the matter." And *there* may even be used to express a battery of emotions: "*There* now," "*There, there*," "*There!* Take that, you scoundrel!" "*There*, that's finally done." None of this has anything to do with *they're*, which is a contraction of *they are*: "*They're* over *there* with *their* entourage."

theirselves   -5 VOQ

Theirselves is an illiterate utterance. The standard word is *themselves*.

thief / burglar / robber

See *burglar / robber / thief*.

thusly   -4 VOQ

We are so accustomed to adverbs ending in *-ly* that it seems only natural to add *-ly* to *thus thusly: thusly*. The problem is that *thus* is already an adverb. The *-ly* is not only superfluous, it is wrong.

tic / tick   -2 VOQ

Tic has but one meaning: a habitual and involuntary muscular contraction, usually of the face or extremities. *Tick* has a host of meanings, including the light, sharp sound of a clock or other clock-like machines, the act of counting or checking something off ("*Tick* off the names as I read them to you, please"), a tiny bloodsucking arachnid of the family *Ixodidae*, and the cloth case for a mattress or pillow.

timber / lumber   -3 VOQ

Timber is a collective noun signifying trees or a forested area regarded as a source of wood. *Lumber* is wood that has been cut and milled into standard sizes for purposes of construction. The two terms are distinct and not interchangeable; however, *timber* is sometimes used to denote major structural elements in older or traditionally built houses, wooden ships ("shiver me *timbers*"), or other massive wooden structures, such as bridges: "The roof *timbers* are magnificent."

timber / timbre   -3 VOQ

Timbre, the quality of a sound that distinguishes it from other sounds of the same pitch and volume, may be pronounced "tam-ber" or "timber," and because of the second pronunciation, it is sometimes spelled *timber*. Most authorities find this unacceptable. Avoid it, and favor the "tam-ber" pronunciation.

toothsome   -3 VOQ

One would think this word had been modeled, say, on *buxom*, to describe a person or animal with many teeth. Alas, the word means neither more nor less than delicious.

tortuous / torturous -3.5 VOQ

Miss Nomer admits, it *is* difficult to avoid confusing these
words. But let's try, shall we? *Tortuous* means twisting. A
tortuous road is a roundabout route characterized by an abundance of hairpin turns. By metaphorical extension, "*tortuous*
logic" is a line of argument that is twisted and complex,
perhaps purposely devious. *Torturous* has a second *r* that
makes it sound more like *torture*, which is appropriate, since
it describes something that produces pain or involves torture:
"I had a *torturous* experience in the dentist's chair."

toward / towards -1.5 VOQ

In American English, the preferred form of this word is *toward*. In British English, *towards* takes the honors.

toxin / tocsin -2 VOQ

A *toxin* is a poison, and a *tocsin* is an alarm or the bell used
to sound an alarm. Figuratively, *tocsin* may mean a warning
or an ill omen.

tragedy / tragic -2.5 VOQ

The noun and its associated adjective are subject to verbal
inflation—that is, they are used so often that they have lost
much of their value and force. *Tragedy,* in its strictest sense,
is about the downfall of the great and mighty as a result of
a fatal flaw in the character of the victim. Sticklers prefer
that *tragedy* and *tragic* be applied only in this strict sense.
Perhaps they are right, perhaps not. But certainly these terms
should be used only to describe a situation in which something valiant, heroic, or great is involved: "The firefighter

ventured without hesitation into the blazing building to rescue the girl. The collapse of the building at that point was
tragic.'' Avoid ''The collapse of your wonderful soufflé was
tragic.''

transpire   -4 VOQ

This word is misused more often than it is used correctly.
To *transpire* is to be emitted as a vapor. For example, vapor
containing waste materials *transpires* through the stomata or
pores of plant tissue. Figuratively, *transpire* may also mean
to become known, to come to light, to leak out, in the sense
of secret information leaking out: ''Despite his best efforts
to hide the truth, it finally *transpired* that he had met with
his company's chief competitor.'' Time and again, however,
the word is misused as a synonym for *happen* or *occur* or
come to pass: ''At what time did these events *transpire*?''
This is incorrect.

traveled / travelled / traveler / traveller / traveling / travelling   -2 VOQ

In modern American English, these words are spelled with
one *l*. *Travelled, traveller,* and *travelling* are favored in Britain, but seem archaic on this side of the Atlantic.

treasure trove   -2 VOQ

A *trove* is not a vault, cache, or storage place. It comes from
an Anglo-Norman word meaning *find*, and thus it means a
find or discovery. Careful writers and speakers will therefore
want to avoid, as redundant, sentences like this one: ''We
found a *treasure trove*.''

trivia   -3 VOQ

Treat this word as what it is: plural. "I am not concerned
with this *trivia*" should be "these *trivia.*"

troop / troupe   -2 VOQ

A *troop* is a group or band of people, animals, or even things,
although the term is most familiar in the sense of a military
unit. Add an *s*, and you have either a plural denoting more
than one unit or a synonym for *soldiers*. The singular *troop*
is not a synonym for *soldier*, however; *trooper* comes closer
to this. *Troop* may also function as a verb, meaning to go in
a group: "Let's all *troop* down to the corner and wait."
Troupe, a French spelling of *troop*, means, in English, a company of entertainers—actors, singers, dancers—and a
trouper is either a member of such a company, a veteran
actor, or, by extension, any tireless and uncomplaining
worker.

true fact   -3.5 VOQ

This phrase comes to us direct from the Department of Redundancy Department. By definition, a fact is true. Avoid
absurdity by avoiding this silly phrase. Also see *free gift*.

try and   -3.5 VOQ

"Will I visit you? *Try and* stop me!" Use *to* rather than *and*,
which is a tired colloquialism.

turbid / turgid −4 VOQ

These words sound alike, but they convey unrelated meanings. Applied to liquid, *turbid* means murky, clouded, or muddy. *Turgid* cannot be applied to liquid. It means bombastic, inflated, excessively complex: "The software manual was written in *turgid* prose." A secondary sense is physical, meaning swollen or distended.

turpitude / rectitude −4 VOQ

They both end in *-tude*, but they mean opposite things. *Turpitude* usually follows the word *moral* and means depravity or utter baseness. *Rectitude* means, literally, the quality of uprightness, and thus moral *rectitude* is the opposite of moral *turpitude*.

twerp / twirp −1 VOQ

The word rhymes with *chirp*, so *twirp* looks like the better choice; nevertheless, the preferred spelling is *twerp*.

type −3.5 VOQ

"This *type* behavior is unacceptable." So is this *type of* sentence. *Type* is primarily a noun and, as such, must be followed by *of*. However, it can be used to transform a noun into a hyphenated compound adjective—"He was a Lenny Bruce–*type* comedian"—provided that the resulting compound adjective is very specific.

U

ukelele / ukulele   -3 VOQ

A small minority of authorities are willing to accept *ukelele* as a variant of *ukulele*, but most regard it as a common misspelling, period. Write *ukulele*.

unanimous   -4 VOQ

Unanimous can never be used as a comparative. It is absolute and absolutely means total agreement; therefore, "more *unanimous*," "less *unanimous*," and "more or less *unanimous*" are all incorrect.

under water / underwater   -3 VOQ

"The wreck was *under water* and was explored by an expert in *underwater* photography." Make these two words one only if you need an adjective.

under way / underway   -1.5 VOQ

The preferred form is two words, not one: "Let's get this job *under way*."

uninterested

See *disinterested / uninterested*.

unique
-4 VOQ

Unique means one of a kind, period. It does not mean special or unusual; therefore, such frequently heard expressions as "He has a more *unique* style than anyone else" are meaningless. Either a thing is either unique—one of a kind—or it isn't. There is no room for degree.

unless and until
VOQ -3

"We will follow routine practice *unless and until* the situation changes." What happens if you delete *and until*? To the meaning of the sentence, absolutely nothing. To the elegance and efficiency of the prose, a substantial improvement. Cast off excess baggage.

unloosen / loosen

See *loosen / unloosen*.

unravel / ravel

See *ravel / unravel*.

up until
-2 VOQ

Why not just say *until*?

use to
-5 VOQ

This illiteracy is born of poor hearing, poor articulation, or a combination of the two. The correct phrase is *used to*: "We *used to* visit my aunt quite frequently."

utilize -3 VOQ

Some words are like blowfish. At the slightest provocation they puff up. *Utilize* is a word form favored by self-important pseudo-technical people. *You*, of course, are better than that. Here's a simple rule: Wherever *utilize* can be used, use *use* instead. This is true for the word in all its forms: *utilizes / uses*; *utilized / used*; *utilizing / using*.

vacant / vacuous -2 VOQ

Vacant means empty or unoccupied. Applied to individuals, it may mean lacking intelligence or lacking expression, as in "a *vacant* stare." *Vacuous* signifies something that is devoid of meaning or sense: "His comment was utterly *vacuous*, and his mind quite *vacant*."

valedictorian / salutatorian / valetudinarian -2.5 VOQ

Valedictorian is frequently misused to identify any student speaker in a commencement exercise. The *valedictorian*, the student who ranks academically highest in the graduating class, is accorded the honor of delivering the closing—valedictory—speech in the ceremony. The *salutatorian*, who ranks second in the class, delivers the welcoming address, which opens the ceremony. A *valetudinarian*, in contrast to both of these words, is unconcerned with academic performance and isn't even in class, because he's overly, even morbidly, concerned with the state of his health. *Valetudi-*

narian is almost a synonym for *hypochondriac*, but it can also be used to denote a person who suffers from genuine chronic ill health.

varied / various -3 VOQ

These are not interchangeable. *Varied* means variegated, made different, or made *various*. *Various* is simply a synonym for *diverse*. "The fabrics *varied* in shade from beet red to light pink. We were shown *various* swatches."

variously -3 VOQ

"Lincoln was seen *variously* as a tyrant and a hero." The problem with this sentence is that *variously* cannot be used with fewer than three things at issue. Had the writer put it this way, "Lincoln was seen *variously* as a tyrant, a crude backwoodsman, and a hero," *variously* would have served him well. The first sentence could be rewritten thus: "Some called Lincoln a tyrant, others a hero."

vault / safe -3 VOQ

A *vault* is not a *safe*, not even a big *safe*. Although usually heavy, a *safe* is either portable or at least movable, whereas a *vault* is permanently and immovably built into the building that houses it. Size is also a difference. One can usually walk into a *vault* but not into a *safe*.

venal / venial -3 VOQ

Words that turn upon a single vowel are easy to mix up. *Venal* is an adjective applied to persons, institutions, and governments that are open to bribery and corruption, whereas *venial* is an adjective applied to transgressions and, by the Catholic church, to sins that are minor and easily forgiven. "His *venial* nature was responsible for a string of sins that were by no means merely *venial*."

verbal / oral

See *oral / verbal*.

verdict   -4 VOQ

Question: "What was the judge's *verdict*?"

Answer: The judge rendered no *verdict*, because only a jury can do this. The pronouncements of a judge are judgments, decisions, findings, rulings, and opinions. Never *verdicts*.

via   -4 VOQ

"We traveled *via* jet, landed in Chicago, then ended up in New York." Well, not really. You traveled *in* a jet, *via* Chicago, to New York. *Via* properly refers not to the means of conveyance but to the route: not *via* car but "in a car *via* old Route 66."

vice / vise   -2.5 VOQ

The meaning of *vice* ranges from a bad habit such as smoking cigarettes to a felony such as prostitution, gambling, or pornography. Far more innocent is *vise*, which denotes a clamp used to hold an object in place so that it can be drilled, sanded, planed, or otherwise worked with tools.

vicinity of, in the
-2 VOQ

This is the long way around saying *near*. Why waste gas on this detour?

viral / virulent
-3.5 VOQ

Only one of these adjectives, *viral*, pertains directly to a virus. A *viral* disease is one that is caused by a virus. *Virulent* means highly infectious; the source of the infection may be a virus, a bacterium, or some other agent. Figuratively, *virulent* also means extremely hostile, bitterly hostile, extremely severe, or scathing, as in "*virulent* criticism."

virtual, virtually
-2 VOQ

Thanks to the personal computer, the concept of *virtual* reality—that is, electronically simulated reality—has become widely known, and the terms *virtual* and *virtually* are now greatly overused. Nowadays one encounters these terms *virtually* anyplace where *almost* or *practically* would do just as well or even better. Words that suffer from severe overuse create annoyance, and annoyance is antithetical to persuasion, which is what oral and written communication is all about.

virus
-2 VOQ

"I have a *virus*" is a careless way of saying that you have a cold or the flu or you just don't feel well. If your illness were bacterial in nature, would you say "I have a germ"? It is best to avoid this expression and say "I have the flu" or "I have a viral infection."

voluptuary / voluptuous   -3 VOQ

To be *voluptuous* is to be ample in form, curvaceous, suggesting sensual pleasure: "Peter Paul Rubens delighted in painting the *voluptuous* figures of women." *Voluptuous* may also describe one who is devoted to sensual pleasure. In either case, *voluptuous* is always an adjective, whereas *voluptuary* is a noun, meaning a person who has entirely given his or her life over to luxury and the enjoyment of sensual pleasures: "After winning the lottery, John became a shameless *voluptuary*."

vulnerable / susceptible

See *susceptible / vulnerable*.

W

wait for / wait on   -3.5 VOQ

Wait on in the sense of *serve* is accepted as standard English, but *wait on* as an alternative to *wait for* is considered nonstandard and should be avoided.

waiver / waver   -3.5 VOQ

Waiver is a noun, and *waver* is a verb. A *waiver* is an act by which one voluntarily relinquishes—*waives*—one's right to something, such as the right to sue in a particular instance. The word also applies to the document that is the instrument of the *waiver*. To *waver* is to move unsteadily back and forth.

This may be an actual physical motion, or it may be figurative: "Be firm. Don't *waver* on this simple issue of right versus wrong."

wean   -4 VOQ

Wean means to end dependence on mother's milk. The word may be applied to human or other mammalian infants. Figuratively, *wean* may be used to express the end of some other dependence or influence: "By the age of eight, I had been *weaned* from comic books and had begun reading adventure novels." Notice the preposition *from*. It is important, because one is *weaned from*, not *weaned on*. "I was *weaned on* Nancy Drew mysteries" is an incorrect use of the word. *Wean* does not mean *reared, raised, nurtured,* or otherwise *nourished*. If you reject the preposition *on* in favor of *from*, you will always avoid the mistake of confusing *wean* with these or similar words.

wharf / dock / pier

See *dock / pier / wharf*.

whereabouts   -3 VOQ

Despite the *s* at the end of this word, it should be treated as a singular: "Her *whereabouts* is unknown." For some speakers and writers, this may take getting used to.

whether / if

See *if / whether*.

which

See *that / which*.

while / and   -2 VOQ

While has two major meanings: *during the time that* and *although* or *but*. "Wait here *while* I ask a question" and "*While* you are right about the first point, you are mistaken about the second" are both correct uses of *while*. But consider this: "The computer is equipped with the latest microprocessor, *while* the monitor is also of the latest design." The problem here is that *while* is used in the sense of neither "during the time that" nor "although." It functions here as a substitute for *and*. Why? There is no good reason to use *while* when *and* is called for.

whiskey / whisky   -1 VOQ

Which spelling is correct? The answer depends on where you are and what kind of booze you're talking about. Americans and the Irish spell it this way: *whiskey*. The Scots and the Canadians spell it without the *e*: *whisky*. It follows, then, that if you are writing of American or Irish spirits, *whiskey* is correct: "bourbon *whiskey*," "sour mash *whiskey*," "Irish *whiskey*." If you are writing about Scotch, it's *whisky*, laddie, and the same is true of Canadian *whisky*.

who / whom   -4 VOQ

Few little words in our language make as much trouble as this pair. The rule governing the choice of *who* or *whom* is simple: Use *who* when the nominative case is called for and *whom* when you need an object. The rule is simple, but it is not always so easy to tell when the nominative case is required and when the pronoun serves as an object.

Let's start with the clearest instance. Whenever the pronoun immediately follows a preposition and is not the subject of a clause, use *whom*: "To *whom* did you give the letter?" "This was intended for *whom*?" "Sarah is taller than *whom*?" However: "Give this to *whoever* is there" is correct because *whoever* is the subject of the clause.

But what happens when things get more complicated?

Don't despair, and don't perform a complicated grammatical analysis, either. Just take the complex sentence under consideration and turn it into a more straightforward sentence: "Sarah Coates, *whom* (or *who?*) Chairman Meyerson nominated for assistant clerk, was not present at the meeting." Simplify: "Meyerson nominated *her*." *Her* is in the objective case; therefore, *whom* is called for. Here's another: "Sarah Coates, *whom* (or *who?*) Chairman Meyerson decided is the best candidate for assistant clerk, was not present at the meeting." If you simplify this one, you get "Meyerson decided *she* was the best candidate." *She* is nominative; therefore, *who* is called for.

who's / whose   -3 VOQ

The little apostrophe creates big problems for many speakers and writers. Sometimes it indicates possession, and sometimes it indicates a contraction. That's confusing enough, but in the case of *who's* and *whose*, which are pronounced identically, the apostrophe is used to indicate a contraction, but is not used to indicate possession. Don't look for a logical reason. Just get it right. *Who's* is a contraction of *who is*, whereas *whose* is a possessive pronoun: "*Whose* briefcase is it?" "It belongs to John, *who's* standing over there."

Let's pursue *whose* a step further. You will still find lunatic usage "experts" who insist that *whose* must be used only with persons and never with things. Such self-proclaimed mavens would reject, for instance, a sentence like this: "The car, *whose* tires were flat, was going nowhere." They would insist instead on: "The car, the tires of which were flat, was going nowhere." This is unwieldy and intolerable. *Whose* may be used for things as well as persons. It is well worth enduring a raised eyebrow to escape the absurd contortions required to avoid *whose*.

widow of the late . . .   -4 VOQ

This absurd redundancy is frequently encountered: "Mrs. DePeyster, *widow of the late* Seymour DePeyster . . ." The sole requirement for widowhood is a dead husband. *Widow of the late* is as silly as speaking of a "round circle."

win   -2 VOQ

Avoid using this word as a noun—"He scored a *win*"— when more vivid noun alternatives are available: "He scored a *victory*."

witch   -2 VOQ

Aside from the danger of confusing *witch* with *which,* you should know that not everyone considers *witch* a wholly negative word denoting an evil, and usually ugly, female practitioner of sorcery. A *witch* may also be a believer and follower of Wicca, a pagan religion practiced mostly in England but also in the United States and, to a lesser extent, elsewhere.

with the exception of   -3 VOQ

Trim this down to *except* or *except for*.

witness   -3 VOQ

Often carelessly used as a grander-sounding substitute for
see, this word does not mean precisely the same thing as *see*.
One can *see* anything: an object, a person, or an event. Properly used, however, *witness* is reserved for seeing events.
You *see* the Empire State Building, but you *witness* a purse-
snatching there. (Hey, relax. It could happen anywhere!)

woman's rights / women's rights   -3 VOQ

Use the plural in this phrase, but the particular right of the
ballot for women is always called *woman suffrage*.

worst comes to worst   -0.5 VOQ

Listen closely, and you will hear this cliché uttered three
different ways:

> If *worst comes to worst* . . .

> If *worse comes to worse* . . .

> If *worse comes to worst* . . .

No less an authority than Theodore M. Bernstein, in *The
Careful Writer*, declares that the phrase has been *worst comes
to worst* since the seventeenth century, and the standard dictionaries agree that this illogical phrase is correct usage. Perhaps a single eyebrow of some twisted little person will rise

if you depart from *worst*, but either of the other expressions makes more sense than the accepted standard. It's up to you.

would of   -5 VOQ

This is an illiterate mistake. The correct phrase is *would have*, which may be contracted to *would've*.

wrack / rack

See *rack / wrack*.

Xerox / xerox   -1.5 VOQ

At the office, do you ask for a photocopy or a *xerox*? If you feel a sneeze coming on, do you ask for a tissue or a *kleenex*? Some trademarks get so familiar that they are transformed into generic terms. If a company does not take vigorous action to counter this (as, for example, the Xerox Corporation did during the 1980s in a long and expensive series of television and print ads), it runs the risk of losing its trademark protection. Familiar words like *Xerox* and *Kleenex* are trademarks and are therefore treated as proper nouns. They must be capitalized. Better yet, use the appropriate generic equivalent, such as *photocopy* or *tissue*.

Z

zoom down

Technically, you cannot *zoom down*, but only *up*, or, if you are using, say, a video camera with a zoom lens, you may *zoom in* and *zoom out*. What you can do downward is *swoop*. Just don't try to *swoop up*.